SEP 18 1990

retail advertising copy:
the how
the what
the why

judy young ocko

published by
Sales Promotion/Marketing Division
NATIONAL RETAIL MERCHANTS ASSOCIATION
100 West 31st St.,   New York, N. Y. 10001

Revised Edition

Copyright, 1971, by

National Retail Merchants Association

100 West 31st Street, New York, N.Y. 10001

Copyright also under the Universal Copyright Convention; copyright in Great Britain, Canada; and in all countries which are members of the International Copyright Union; also copyright in all countries which are signatory to the Copyright Conventions of Montevideo, Mexico, Rio de Janeiro, Buenos Aires and Havana.

ALL RIGHTS RESERVED. NO PART OF THIS BOOK MAY BE REPRODUCED IN ANY FORM, BY MIMEOGRAPH OR ANY OTHER MEANS, WITHOUT PERMISSION IN WRITING FROM THE PUBLISHERS.

Printed in the United States of America

Sixth Printing 1984

```
659.1322 O16r 1971

Ocko, Judy Young.

Retail advertising copy
```

Library of Congress Catalogue Card No. 70-174760

FOREWORD

Seldom does a book reach a sixth printing. Yet, this sixth printing of Retail Advertising Copy: The How, The What, The Why continues to line the shelves of retail ad departments and advertising agencies. Often used as a college text, Judy Young Ocko has contributed a standard guide here, for copywiters everywhere.

This writing is not, however, limited to only advertising practitioners. Store managers and visual merchandising directors, (anyone seeking to upgrade their marketing skills), have found the following pages a valuable reference. You will, too. And one day you'll be recommending the seventh, and quite possibly, eighth printings.

JOHN A. MURPHY
Vice President

Sales Promotion/Marketing Division
National Retail Merchants Association

TABLE OF CONTENTS

INTRODUCTION

CHAPTER 1. COPY IS SALESMANSHIP
    the difference between copy and other forms of writing........ 1

CHAPTER 2. COPY IS NEWS
    the different forms of copy 5

CHAPTER 3. WHERE DO IDEAS COME FROM?
    how to get an ad started 9

CHAPTER 4. THE AD: WHAT IT CONSISTS OF
    the elements of an ad 15

CHAPTER 5. THE TOOLS OF THE TRADE
    type, newspapers, reference works 20

CHAPTER 6. THE TRICKS OF THE TRADE
    guiding principles for better copy 25

CHAPTER 7. THE DEMONS
    legal and other restrictions on copy 30

CHAPTER 8. WATCH YOUR LANGUAGE
    how to make words work for you 33

CHAPTER 9. THE DO'S AND THE DON'TS
    basic rules for copywriters 39

CHAPTER 10. THE VERSUS PROBLEM
    various approaches to copy.. 43

CHAPTER 11. THE BIGGEST SALE EVER
    how to write strong sale copy 48

CHAPTER 12. THE IMAGE
    how to project a store's personality in copy 52

CHAPTER 13. THE CAMPAIGN
    from conception to execution 59

CHAPTER 14. CHRISTMAS COMES EVERY YEAR
    the annual events and sales 63

CHAPTER 15. THE OTHER STORES
   specialized forms of copy 70
CHAPTER 16. MEET THE PRESS
   how to write press releases and special event ads ... 75
CHAPTER 17. YOU AND THE ART DEPARTMENT
   a copywriter's guide to layout and art 79
CHAPTER 18. RADIO: LEND US YOUR EARS
   how to write radio commercials 83
CHAPTER 19. TV: "THE MEDIUM IS NOT THE MESSAGE"
   how to write TV commercials 93
CHAPTER 20. PLEASE SEND ME
   direct mail and how to write it 100
CHAPTER 21. MARKETING
   the new retail advertising tool 108
CHAPTER 22. A COPYWRITER'S LOT
   the other things a writer writes 110
CHAPTER 23. STORE NAME GOES HERE
   how to make co-op copy your own 117
CHAPTER 24. MONEY, MONEY, MONEY!
   who pays for the advertising 121
CHAPTER 25. THE TALK OF THE TRADE
   a brief dictionary of advertising language 124
CHAPTER 26. BE STRONG, BE PROFESSIONAL
   advice to copywriters 129
CHAPTER 27. POSTSCRIPT FOR STUDENTS
   how to get your first job 132
INDEX 133
ABOUT THE AUTHOR 136

INTRODUCTION

Not every book needs revision, but a book on copy does. Because copy ages a lot faster than wine. When I reread this book a few months ago, some of the language and all of the prices in the examples sounded quaint. There had been major changes in newspapers and minor changes in just about everything else.

In the past twelve years, I've talked to a lot of people who work for smaller stores. The things they wanted to know, from public relations to advertising language and proofreaders' marks, have now become part of the text.

If you own the first edition, you'll find four completely new chapters here, and big additions to many others. Otherwise, well, this is all about retail advertising copy today. Until another revision comes along.

Judy Young Ocko

PREFACE

In my years as a copywriter, the first question I've learned to ask myself when I sit down at a typewriter is this: to whom am I talking? Who is the "you"?

In this book, the "you" can be any one of an interesting array of people. You can be a copywriter, novice or pro, who wants to be a more effective writer. Or a copy chief with writers to train.

You can be working in a store, an agency, in broadcast, in direct mail, or a newspaper . . because the principles behind good copy are, happily, the same. Or you can be a student preparing for any of these jobs.

You can be a merchant or an account executive who'd like to put into words why you do or do not like an ad.

You can be an art director or layout artist who has to talk to copywriters in their own language.

You can be an advertising manager for a giant company . . or the owner of a small store that advertises once in a while.

In short, if you come face to face with advertising in any role, this book is addressed to you . . and you . . and you. For, in writing it, I discovered that, just as copy can't be written in a vacuum, neither can it be explained in a vacuum. In order to give its principles, I also had to present its philosophy: the reasons why copy is written the way it is. As a result, this book is about advertising in a broad sense, as well as copy.

I hope you find it profitable.

Judy Young Ocko

CHAPTER 1
COPY IS SALESMANSHIP

What is a Copywriter?

A copywriter is not just a person with a knack for words, although we must know our way around words.

A copywriter is not just a long-haired creative artist, although the more creative we are, the better we are.

Instead, a copywriter is actually a salesman behind a typewriter. We use our typewriters to sell, sell, sell. Whether we are promoting an idea or an item, whether we're writing hard-hitting prose that screams SALE or salutes the Red Cross in chaste language, we are always selling our store.

Selling via copy is more difficult than selling over the counter. For one thing, you're trying to persuade thousands instead of one person. For another, copy is a monologue instead of a dialogue. You are talking to an unseen audience that you must grab and hold and inspire to action.

What is Copy?

How does it differ from reporting, straight writing?

Reporters give facts: the whole truth and nothing but the truth. They tell the who, why, what, where and when without adding opinion, guesses, personality, or imagination. They are not concerned with the reader's motivation, not interested in creating a mood. Instead, they let the facts speak for themselves.

Straight writers add imagination to reportorial skills. Novelists, playwrights, poets, or even writers of non-fiction, they create character and mood, give every piece of writing the imprint of their own personalities. They use facts, rather than relating them. They put flesh on the bones of data. They exaggerate, slant, angle, always from a specific point of view.

Copywriters are part reporter, part straight writer. While they must stick to the facts, they add mood, understand motivation, enhance without exaggerating. They, too, have a point of view. However, it's not their own point of view, but the point of view of the store for which they work. Primarily, copywriters are salesmen, using their writing skills to sell. They give all the facts, but interpret them for the reader . . the customer. Every word, every sentence, every paragraph must add up to a selling message. They must create the desire to buy, leave the reader with an urge to take action. They must marshal their facts so the ultimate conclusion is a sale . . even if what's being sold is an image rather than a product.

What is Good Copy?

Since the function of every ad is to sell, the effectiveness of copy can best be measured by its results. This does not mean that every ad should be a door-buster, unless that's the function of your ad. Rather, it means that the ad should do precisely what you want it to do, whether it's moving merchandise or polishing your image.

It's simple enough to measure the results of a one-day sale, but how do you measure the immeasurables? Not today, not next week, but over a period of time.

Abercrombie & Fitch was, for example, for generations a store you only shopped if you were going on a safari or were a devoted (and rich) sportsman. Some years ago A & F decided to broaden the base of their customer appeal. They began a very cleverly written campaign, done in first person. The campaign created a lot of talk, but apparently did not produce the volume of business anticipated. They lost a million dollars in 1969-70.

Now this was intriguing copy, eminently readable, with facts, prices, sales pitch. But it failed its purpose of increasing business, so it cannot be called good copy.

On the other hand, there's a radio campaign that ran for years that made esthetes wince. It started "Today only at Macy*s! 30% (or whatever) off regular prices!" It proceeded like a punch press. And pulled in customers like crazy. It may have offended some ears, but this was good copy. It worked. Happily, it is not the *only* kind of copy that is good. Thousands and thousands of golf balls were sold with an ad headlined "We don't know exactly why, but this new golf ball drives 4 yds. to 12 yds. further . . . every time". Soft sell, regular price . . . and a winner.

Is there any way to pre-test, pre-judge copy? Pre-testing retail copy, the way an agency pre-tests a campaign, is almost impossible for a store. There just isn't time. Today's hotsie is tomorrow's dead duck. But you can TEST YOUR OWN COPY BY ASKING TWO QUESTIONS:

1. **Does my ad include the customer benefits?** Does it answer the question: what will it do for ME? (Like the golf ball ad quoted above.) A customer benefit is really a promise. It will make me look nicer, improve my status. It will impress neighbors, save time, be good for my kids, make my husband think I'm a better wife. Make me a better golfer. And so on. In other words, motivate the sale. If you can get your promise, your primary benefit into the headline, great. Otherwise include it in the copy. It can be explicit or implicit. If your headline reads "The new pouchy handbag", you're promising the customer that, if she buys it, she'll be in fashion. You don't actually have to spell it out.

2. **Does my ad give a reason for buying at my store?** Ideally, every ad should say or imply that your merchandise is the best, the most, the thriftiest, the newest, the most fashionable, or exclusive. ("Only at Blah Blah" may be a bore to write, but this may be the best reason of all, because your customer can't get the goods somewhere else.)

What if your ad is the same old Cannon towel at the same price as every other store in and out of town? Dramatize one part of the story and it becomes your own. Talk Cannon's sunny yellow and let the other colors be also-rans. Find out if there's something in the construction or thread count and make a big deal of it. Take the towel home if necessary and use it and say "We tested it ourselves". Or build your copy around your total collection of Cannon, and let the item be an example of the larger story — that your store is the place to buy Cannon towels.

Giving the customer benefits and the reason for buying at your store will bring people in, provided that you have been honest, and the merchandise is both right and priced right. Unfortunately, even the most convincing, most dramatic, most powerful ad can't move bad goods. The only thing we can be sure of is that a good ad moves more merchandise than a weak ad.

CHAPTER 2
COPY IS NEWS

Ever watch a woman go through a newspaper? She reads the retail ads as though they were news...and to her, they are. They help her in her job of being a woman. They tell her about new products, new fashions, new ways to improve the quality of her life, new ways to save her money.

Write your copy as news. Chances are you'll catch her eye, her interest, and maybe even her dollars. It may take a little digging to get the news out of the merchandise, but worth the effort. Two of the most magical words you can use are "new" and "now". Instead of writing pretty phrases...like "a beautiful bevy of bedspreads" (which doesn't say a thing except that you have bedspreads)...give the news. "Now your bedspread can go from washer to dryer to bed". "Bedspreads in new bold colors". "Bedspreads in new soft colors". "Now quilted bedspreads in queen and king sizes, too".

Newsworthiness is, more and more, the common denominator of all forms of advertising. Gone are the days when a national ad merely patted a company on the back for doing what it had done for the past hundred years.

Substantial differences remain, of course.

The retail ad says come and get it. Now. At my store. At this price. In these colors and sizes. The national ad says next time you're shopping look for me. In any store. Or in the stores listed. A mail order ad is a retail ad, plus everything that makes it possible to order without seeing the merchandise. (We don't have to tell our customers that a dress has a full length back zipper. They can come try it on.)

Retail copy is, in every way, immediate. It talks directly, woman to woman, man to man. And, because it's prepared on a relatively tight schedule (anywhere from 3 hours to 3 weeks in advance), it can relate closely to the things of the moment, the phrases of the hour. Because, as a retail copywriter, you know your audience, you can talk directly to them. You know how they live, what's on their minds, what their problems are, their ambitions, their heroes, their level of sophistication.

One of the frustrations in writing national copy is that great unseen audience. When I wrote cosmetics copy for an agency, this always worried me. How could I appeal to a woman in Atlanta and Butte in the same ad? Sure, they both wanted to be beautiful, but that's the broadest common denominator. Generalities rarely produce good ads. So, next time you eye a national ad and mutter "why don't they say something", remember that perhaps they can't.

Aside from economics, split runs and regional editions of magazines are a great boon. At least you know you're talking to Eastern women, or farm women, or women with incomes over or under $10,000.

Even within retail copy, there are special and different forms. Fashion copy, sale copy, and institutional copy, for example, are each worlds of their own.

Fashion Copy

By definition, this must be news. If it isn't news, it isn't fashion. (Last year's hemline might as well be whalebone corsets.) It also must be more authoritative than other forms of copy. We are telling our customers we have the right thing to wear now. And, strangely enough, it can be more impersonal and less warm than other copy. Fashion, no matter how light-hearted, is a serious matter and a woman doesn't want you to cozy up to her on the subject. There's some big third party out there settling matters. "They" are wearing it. "They" say belts are coming in. Who are "they"? Who knows, but "they" are never wrong!

Obviously then, fashion copy must give the fashion news. It

must also give it in such a way that the merchandise sounds irresistible. Here is the place to be bright, clever, seductive. And brief. For your art work does most of the job for you. You don't have to mention the buttons and belts (they can see them) unless buttons and belts are this year's fashion points. On the other hand, you'd better be pretty specific about a broiler that broils, toasts, bakes, and fries. Because you are selling not what the broiler is, but what it does.

Sale Copy

Sale copy may be the most misunderstood and underrated copy on earth. Sale copy does not mean writing an ad and saying SALE. Or putting the price in 72-point type and adding "regularly $00".

A sale should sell the savings plus the merchandise. You must make clear to the reader why it's such a buy at the price. You don't have to do this when you're selling eggs at 22¢ a dozen. The value is communicated immediately. But when you're selling a pair of pants for $19 that were $25 yesterday, you'd better make them sound like more than $19-worth.

More than your money's worth is the real key to powerful sale advertising. Everybody loves a bargain. If you make the bargain sound believable, you've got your audience. How do you do it? See Chapter 11.

Institutional Copy

The other special world of retail newspaper advertising is the institutional, or if I may un-polysyllabify it, the ad that sells your store or some part of your store. When you face your typewriter to write an institutional, you don't sit down to dream and create. Like any other ad, you start with a point of view. What is this ad supposed to do? You start with facts and build your story on them.

An institutional can be as unrelated to merchandise as saluting a festival your city is putting on. It can be the opening of a new store, a new floor. It can be a special event. It can be a store service like credit or returns. It can launch an anniversary sale. It can be a Merry Christmas to all. Or it can tell a new merchandise story. And everything in between.

No matter what the subject matter, the ad must do something for your store. It must reflect the store's style, the personality of the store. For many years, Macy*s ran about an ad a week, hailing and building audiences for the exciting things that made New York a great city: shows, movies, ballet, music, educational TV, scouts, libraries, etc. Mr. Jack Straus was asked what all this had to do with Macy*s. He answered "What's good for New York is good for Macy*s".

This is sound philosophy. A store is as viable as the area it serves. The practical results of the institutionals, however, were two. By associating a store with the fascinating things going on, some of the excitement rubs off on the store. There's also an opportunity to expose facets of the store that never get into print...a "message".

Can you measure the results of an institutional ad? Yes and no. You can count the bodies that turn up for your Winter Carnival. Or, when you run an ad on charge accounts and get over 6,000 coupons back, you know your ad was read. Otherwise, you must rely on the impression people have of your store and the reputation you have carefully cultivated.

CHAPTER 3
WHERE DO IDEAS COME FROM?

Call them what you will; ideas, points of view, angles, approaches. Every ad that is more than a mere listing of facts has one, whether it's a sale of sofas or an institutional hailing a hero.

Where do these ideas come from? Most definitely not out of nowhere, but from the writer's experience: from living, reading, looking, talking. To a writer, experience is like a bank account. The more you have stowed away, the more you have to draw from, because the more a writer knows, sees, or feels, the easier it is to write.

This generality, to be sure, applies to all writers, not just copywriters. The ability to turn experience, first or even second hand, into ideas is the distinguishing characteristic of a writer. Mind you, ideas, not words. A string of beautiful words will not make an ad...or a poem. *The words must communicate an idea.*

The copywriter draws on two sources of experience, usually at the same time. One is personal experience; the other is store experience...or merchandise experience.

Personal experience is obvious and intangible, so we'll deal with it briefly. It varies, depending on your past...on childhood, background, education, exposure. And it continues every moment of the day.

You vacation in Mexico. The next week, the next month, or the next season, you're describing a dress that's suitable for suburbs or travel. Your experience translates this into "equally at home in the supermarket or sightseeing in Mexico". (Yes, you've been in supermarkets, too.) You go to an art auction and are surrounded by well-dressed women of no uncertain age. The next ad you write for women's fashions says, "It's Smart to be Sixty". You're writing an institutional for an institution...Red Cross, U.S. Savings Bonds, your local library..and you know your Latin. You say "A monument more lasting than bronze". (Horace is public domain.)

On my first job, I recall trying to find a fresh word for "huge quantity". I found it, because I'd just read a book on astronomy. I said "Galaxies of housewares". Today I wouldn't use such a word; it's too reached-for. Amusingly enough, other writers picked it up, and for a while the New York Times was galvanized by galaxies.

To a writer, this is as automatic as breathing. However, it usually provides only the grace notes on copy, the personality and flavor rather than the basic selling idea. This, more often than not, comes out of the merchandise, the writer's store experience, as well as the point of view of the store. (Can you imagine, for example, a discount store and a fine specialty shop running the identical ad on furs? They'd both talk fashion, but their points of view and personalities would be light years apart). For to a good copywriter it's the feel, the touch, the look, the smell of merchandise that starts the ideas rolling.

Let's be specific. Put yourself behind a typewriter for a moment. You're about to write a sale ad on tablecloths and have accumulated these facts:

   pure Irish linen
   drip-dry finish, soil releasing
   2" hems, hemstitched all around
   6 sizes, from 52 x 52 to 60 x 108, including 72" round
   dark green, brown, plum, deep purple, black
   52 x 52" size is 12.98, reg. 17.98; matching napkins
   1.99, reg. 2.99
   nothing else like it around town, because it was made to your store's specifications in Ireland.

How many ideas can you dig out of these facts, each one a sound selling idea on which to build your ad? All the facts are important, but you can't give them all equal emphasis. Which one or ones are the most important to your customer?

Before you start counting on your fingers, be warned. Some of the ideas depend on what you know about tablecloths..on your merchandise experience.

There are at least 9 ideas, other than SALE, hiding in the facts:
1. the luxury of pure Irish linen
2. the convenience of no ironing
3. the low price
4. the hemstitched hems (unusual at the price)
5. the range of sizes (unusual in a sale)
6. the deep colors (unusual in a collection of linens)
7. unique..nothing like them around town (unusual in linens which run pretty much the same)
8. exclusive..your own imports
9. your usual low price is even lower now.

The parenthetical (unusual) is a fact you cannot interpret.. or expound...if you have no merchandise experience. You just wouldn't know. Nor would you know that soil-release drip-dry is relatively new in Irish linens. It's as simple as that. On the same principle, if you don't know that percale sheets usually have 180 threads to the square inch, how can you appreciate the superiority of a sheet with 220 threads? If you've never seen a bolero, how can you write about the *new* boleros?

The most sacred law of copywriting is never NEVER write an ad without first seeing the merchandise. A spec sheet or a photograph or a vendor's ad is no substitute for the real thing. Having looked at (and handled if possible) the merchandise, you then start searching for facts. Here you hit a dilemma, just like looking for a job and being told you need experience. How do you get the experience if you can't get a job?

The problem is this: some buyers are articulate and will bend your willing ear. Others, too many others, are just this side of tongue-tied. You have to pull the facts out of them. To do this, it's necessary to know what questions to ask. But if you don't know anything..or little..about the merchandise, how do you ask questions? Fortunately, there are a few leading questions you can ask without knowing a thing:

Why did you buy it?
Is there anything special about it?
What are the customer benefits?
How does it differ from others on the market?
Why should customers buy it?
Why should customers buy it here?

Ideas grow from facts, but you don't limit yourself to this. You listen with a third ear, watch with a third eye. An artist says something, or a layout suggests an idea, a treatment. For example, Walter Einsel and his wife Naiad, both imaginative artists, baked a giant Macy-shaped cookie one year and suggested we use it for our Christmas ad. We did, photographing the cookie. The copy, naturally, was based on the cookie idea.

Sometimes a buyer gives you a seemingly irrelevant fact, and an ad can be built around it. This happened once when we were planning a layette ad. The writer asked the buyer if young women still brought their mothers with them when they shopped for layettes. She answered yes..and added that she also did a great business in office gifts: girls buying layettes for a colleague leaving to have a baby. The ad was built completely on this idea. It showed, as the major illustration, the typical envelope passed around an office to collect gift money, complete with "signatures" and verse that didn't quite scan. The headline? "The Layette Committee Meets at Noon".

This was more than a stopper. It gave third party endorsement to the layettes. The customer would reason: if smart business girls buy layettes here, that's where I should buy mine as well. Since most layette advertising is a series of adorable babies, this ad caused much comment, was reprinted widely...and sold lots of merchandise. All from a casual comment by a buyer!

The important thing is to grab ideas, wherever they come from..and say thank you. Then, when the ad is praised, give credit. (Conversely, if the ad is a flop, *you* take the rap and don't even whisper your source. After all, you should be smart enough to know a good idea from a dud.) Nothing will win you fewer friends..and make your job harder to do..than preening yourself in public over an idea that wasn't yours in the first place, no matter how immortal the prose in which you expressed it.

So now you have your idea and your facts. How do you make an ad out of them? You can write a headline that expresses your idea, then list facts in their order of importance. Sorry, that's not copy. It's a spec sheet, something like saying Hamlet is a play in which a man avenges his father's murder. It's true, but it's far from Shakespeare's Hamlet.

Is there, then, a formula? If there were, facts might be programmed into a computer and come out copy...and we'd all be unemployed. A good part of this book deals with the many ways to write better copy, copy that does exactly what you want it to do. If you are diligent, you can probably discover a dozen effective exceptions to almost every one of them. But there is one guiding principle you will never find violated in any good piece of retail copy. It's as close to a formula as exists in our business: *Let the customer identify.* In other words, write to your specific audience in terms of that audience's interest. Know your customer as well as your merchandise. Make the situation real and vivid to her. Take your ideas and translate them into her point of view. Here are a few examples.

Your facts say that a children's play gym is built of 20-gauge steel. You ask the buyer what this means. Is it heavier than other gyms, or what? He says it's so sturdy that even a 200-pounder like himself can sit on it safely. Do you write a headline that says "20-gauge steel play gym"? (How often do you see headlines like this..or extra-sturdy steel something-or-other?) No. You write "Our 200-pound buyer sat on this swing". Why? Because you figure that your customer, like yourself, doesn't know the difference between 15 and 20-gauge steel. Yet she can easily visualize a heavy man stitting on the swing. If it's safe enough for him, it must be safe enough for her small youngsters. You've dramatized the most important sales appeal.

Your facts say "pink evening dress in junior sizes". You look at the dress. It's beautiful. It's young. It's obviously just right for the high school prom in your town. The buyer confirms this, has planned the ad at the time prom-goers would be buying. Do you write "Think pink" or "Pretty for proms" or "Turned on for dancing"? No. You write "Make an entrance he'll never forget". (In advertisingese, this gambit has another name as well. It's called sell the sizzle, not the steak.)

Or, to give you the simplest, most everyday example of all. How much more effective is "Save 30% (what *you* do) than "30% off regular price" (what *we're* doing).

CHAPTER 4

THE AD: WHAT IT CONSISTS OF

The elements of an ad, in various combinations, are the headline, the sub-head or lead-in, the body copy, the details, the captions, the base line.

An ad can consist of all or a few of these parts. An ad can be all headline, all copy, a headline and captions, or whatever best tells your story.

The Headline

Morris L. Rosenblum in his "How to Design Effective Store Advertising" says that you have only 3 seconds to stop the customer who's turning the pages of a newspaper. One headline function is to do exactly that. But you must play fair with the reader. You can't start with a headline about Cupid and Psyche, then go into how they got married and set up a home and, of course, every home needs a garbage can, so they bought a Jones galvanized can, only 6.98 this week at our store. Exaggeration? Take a careful look at your newspapers and magazines and your TV screen and see how close this example skates to the awful truth.

A headline should involve the customer, and give the news. It should be solidly based on the merchandise story. This does not mean your headline can't be as bright, as clever, as intriguing as you can make it.

Once at a Retail Advertising Conference, we played a copy game. We showed a layout of 5 different scarves worn 5 different ways, and asked the audience to submit a brief ad. Here are some of the headlines, and what's wrong or right about them.

EVERYBODY'S WRAPPING UP	Nice, because in conjunction with the art, it gives the fashion news with authority
FROM HEAD TO TOE, 1970 SPRING SHAPES	From head to toe is not only a cliche, but ... scarves for shoes?
TIE ONE ON!	This is a good try, but suggests a dirty book. It doesn't come off.
ONE SCARF CANNOT A SEASON MAKE	Literary headlines are fun, but will customers get this? Also, as a purist I like my quotes pure ... and it is "One swallow maketh not summer"
HOW MANY LIVES HAVE YOU LIVED?	An interesting question, but it has nothing to do with scarves.
70's WRAP UP: SCARVES	Neat, brief, pertinent.
EXCLAMATION POINT: THE ACCESSORY SCARF!	With a page of scarves, the second half is unnecessary, and clunky. No woman runs around looking for an "accessory scarf."
A SCARF FOR EVERY REASON	A good play on words because it tells the story.

How long should a headline be? Ideally, the shorter the better. Just enough to stop the reader and/or give a customer benefit. There's a two word headline Macy*s ran once a year for about a dozen years, and it worked. The ad showed two medicine chests, one filled with national brands, the other with Macy*s-Own Brands. The items were listed, the prices totalled. The headline? "Simple Arithmetic".

On the other hand, your headline can be as long as necessary to be effective.

Some years ago, Macy*s expected a strike, so an ad was prepared to tell customers the store was open and executives were manning the counters. The headline was "If you've ever wanted to tell a Macy vice president how to run the store, this may be your chance". There isn't a word you could cut. Long informative headlines are currently in fashion. In New York, Bloomingdale's and Bonwit Teller are both doing them as I write this. Beautifully but differently.

Sometimes art functions as a headline, so you need no headline at all. A dramatic piece of art can be just as much a stopper as an unforgettable phrase, provided the art performs some of the other functions of a headline: news, benefit, etc.

Do you start with the headline when you're writing an ad? Most writers do. However, this isn't a must. You will often find, when you've written the copy, that you have a great headline buried in it, much better than the one you started with. So, if a headline comes hard, don't worry it. Write your ad, then pull your headline out of the copy.

The Lead-In or Sub-Head

These are grouped together because they perform the same function. In bold type, but smaller than the headline, lead-ins or sub-heads amplify the headline while giving additional information or creating a mood when your headline must be factual.

If your headline tells all, there's no need for either lead-in or sub-head.

Using both is bad graphics. You end up with a sandwich: big headline type between two lines of smaller type.

At the moment, sub-heads and lead-ins are out of fashion. However, they can be extremely useful. If you are committed, for instance, to putting the manufacturer's name in bold type and it's not a significant name, a sub-head will keep everyone happy. Of if, for drama, you want a few bold words as a headline, and they're not sufficient to tell enough of the story to intrigue the customer.

For example: you are writing a page of assorted decanters for Christmas. The format dictates a short headline.

GIFT DECANTERS

Dull, leaden-footed, a label rather than a headline. So you add a sub-head, and change the heading slightly because you can get the gift idea in the sub-head.

CONSIDER THE DECANTER
Possibly the one thing they don't have

Better? Of course. But suppose they're Waterford crystal and you must use the name (you would anyway, it's a great name). You have two choices: change your heading or change your sub-head.

A WATERFORD DECANTER
Possibly the one thing they don't have

or

CONSIDER THE DECANTER
An impressive gift in Waterford crystal

Body Copy

Ideally, every sentence in a piece of copy should be a cliff-hanger. It should make the customer want to read the next. A sentence that slows the reader up, that's so involved it has to be re-read, or is full of priceless (but irrelevant) prose, will turn the reader off immediately.

You have only one chance. If the reader stops and turns the page, your ad might as well not be in the paper. That's why most of this book is dedicated to ways you can keep the reader reading.

The Details

These are the little bugs that seem to clutter up a page: floor line, mail and phone information, credit, store hours, branch stores, etc. They may bore you, but they're important to the customer because they make it easier for her to find the merchandise and shop. Happily these miscellaneous facts are usually separate elements in an ad. There are times, however, when, from the store's point of view, they are as important as the merchandise on the page. Then they blossom out as headlines. "Open Late Every Night This Week". "From our new 2nd floor". "Shop by phone". This is a store decision, and you must abide by it.

The Captions

If all your merchandise information is in the body of your ad, you don't need captions. If it isn't, then write separate captions, but be as brief and succinct as you can. Sizes, colors, fibre content, prices. No flights of fancy.

Base Lines

Once in a while, you have a non-merchandise story that must be told importantly. You can then use a bold line across the bottom of the ad. It may be a store slogan. It may be a "no mail, no phone, hurry in" bit. It may be an institutional or semi-institutional store message. Base lines are not generally used as part of a merchandise story. The exception is when you're making a *general* point about the merchandise. You would not say "Blue green, or yellow drip-dry polyester" in a base line. But you might says "Isn't this the way you want to look this year?" Or even "Isn't this the coat you want this year?" Or "From the collection of treasures in our Antiques Corner".

CHAPTER 5
THE TOOLS OF THE TRADE

Nobody expects a copywriter to be an expert on type, but the more you know about it the better you can understand why an ad is designed the way it is.

One way to learn about type is from your local newspaper people who would be only too glad to show you. Or you can borrow a type book from your production department.

Type comes in an almost bewildering profusion of sizes, weights, and styles. The joker is that, if the newspaper is setting your ad, you can only use the type it owns. Unless you're willing to pay for "hand-set" type, which means sending an ad to a company that specializes in typography. Expensive, too.

Today almost all newspapers are using what's known as cold type. Its full name is phototypography and that's exactly what it is. It's set by computer and photographed. The reason it's called cold type is to contrast it with hot type which was used for centuries. Made of molten metal, hence hot.

Cold type can be set by a typist, playing away at the computer. Some big stores now have their own in-house production centers and, at a few of them, copywriters are given "time" at the computer. They actually write their copy (with a pretty polished draft in hand I hope) and set it at the same time. There will probably be more of this in the future as more and more stores invest in the equipment.

Most type comes in sizes from 6 point to 72 point..point being the standard measurement for type. (There are 72 points to the inch.) Some type goes up to 120 points.

This is 6 point type.

This is 18 point type.

Type larger than 14 point is usually display type, used for headings and base lines. Body copy is set in smaller sizes. Most type comes in light, medium, or bold face (the weight of the type).

Most type comes in lower case and upper case (capital letters) and some type comes not only in Roman but in italic (although not always in all sizes). As far as style is concerned, there are basically classic types and modern types. Classic type faces usually have serifs...the fine cross stroke at the top and bottom of a letter (Serif). Many modern type faces are sans-serif. (Sans-Serif). In each category are many many type families. Only your newspaper can tell you which ones they own. And there's no point asking your layout artist to specify "Obelisk" if the newspaper doesn't own it.

However, you will find that your store uses one or two type faces almost exclusively. This is part of the personality of the ad, the thing people recognize.

The space between lines is called "lead". If there is not enough lead between lines, the copy is hard to read. The larger the type, the more lead you require. Like type itself, lead is measured in points. 1-point lead, 2-point lead, etc.

How to Write to a Character Count

This sounds very complicated, but is elementary. You set up a measure..the number of characters to a line..and follow it. You can hyphenate a word at the end of a line of body copy, but few things look more amateurish than a hyphenated headline. If your art department can't make your headline work without hyphenating it, change a word, change a phrase, or rewrite it.

It's always better to write a character or two fewer to a line than one or two over. The printer can space letters and words, but can't squeeze them. However, a line with lots of l's, i's, or t's can be written a bit longer since these actually take half the space of other letters. Lines with lots of capital letters and m's and w's need more space.

Now here's how you do it.

A block of copy 35 characters wide, 3 lines deep

xxxxxxxxxxxxxxxxxxxxxxxxxxxxxxxxxxx(your measure)

When fitting copy to a specific
space, it is important that you
write precisely the number of char-

A block of copy 20 characters wide, 3 lines deep:

xxxxxxxxxxxxxxxxxxxx

When fitting copy to
a specific space, it
is important that you

Newspaper Sizes

Newspapers are either standard size or tabloid, the tabloid being the smaller.

Width is measured by columns. Not too long ago there were two basic sizes in newspapers. The 8-column standard and the 5-column tabloid. No more. We also have 7 and 9 column standards, 4 and 6 column tabs, and every other possible variation. I mean variation. The New York Times, for example, divides its page into 7 columns for news matter... but 9 columns for advertising! The only way to find out how many columns to your page is to ask your art or your production department. Or your newspaper, of course.

Depth is measured by column inches or column agate lines. 14 lines make an inch.

Most big city papers use lines. Most smaller cities inches. Why? Nobody knows. To get the size of the page (or your ad), you measure the width (the number of columns) by the depth (the number of inches or lines). For example, a page that is 8 columns wide and 300 lines deep is a 2400 line page.

If you measured the same page by inches, since there are 14 agate lines to the inch, it would be 8 columns by 21½ inches, or 172 inches for the page.

Local custom dictates whether you measure in lines or inches. There is no difference. Get the specifications from your local paper.

Reference Works

In addition to an unabridged dictionary, what belongs in the armament of a copywriter?

Roget's Thesaurus. This is fine for looking up synonyms, but if you rely on it too strongly, your ad will smell of the student's lamp. Most writers discover that the Thesaurus starts you thinking, and you come up with the precise word on your own.

Bartlett's Quotations. Here's another good way to start the creative juices working in certain cases, but again it should not be overused. It is a must for checking quotes, even though you're sure. Be doubly sure!

A good one or two volume encyclopedia for fascinating facts.

A current world almanac..ditto.

Fowler's English Usage and a standard grammar.

Your newspaper's style book, if they have one.

A rhyming dictionary.

Eric Partridge's Dictionary of Cliches. This is particularly valuable if you are given to plays on words and phrases.

A fabric dictionary..many of the mills can provide this.

In addition to these, a copywriter should have access to the trade journals like *Women's Wear Daily*, etc. They are not to be used slavishly, since their language is "inside" talk, but to get some understanding of what's what in merchandising across the country. Also, out-of-town newspapers and clipping or ad reproduction services can be a great source of ideas.

The copywriter should also read the popular magazines: *Vogue, Harper's, Seventeen, House & Garden, People,* and such. Because this is what your customer reads. And you can't know the words and ideas that your customer responds to if you're out of touch with what is being sold the customer in the pages of the magazines she studies.

It's also important to read your own newspapers carefully. Partly to see what the competition is doing and partly, again, to know what your reader is reading.

CHAPTER 6
THE TRICKS OF THE TRADE

The You Approach

We write for thousands of people, but the customer reads an ad as though it were written just for her or him.

That's why good copy relies so strongly on the me-to-you point of view.

Ideally, YOU, actual or implied, should be in every headline. For example: "Give them a fondue set for Christmas, and they may invite you back for New Year's". The hortatory "give" has YOU built into it. More subtly: "New York loves the little black dress". I (the reader) live in New York, therefore when you say "New York", you are saying "You love the little black dress".

YOU should also be used throughout the copy, as if you were talking face to face with an actual person. Not "There are 3 ways to wear this bracelet", but "You can even wear this bracelet 3 ways". In other words, personal..not impersonal.

Exceptions: Sometimes your audience is not a YOU. Obviously, when you write snow suits, you talk to mama. Less obviously, when you write gift merchandise, it's not YOU who will use it and enjoy it, but HE or SHE or THEY. Sometimes you deliberately write 3rd person or 1st person copy for a special effect. You can often write a good fashion headline without YOU, but YOU should be in the copy. Fashion is, as usual, different.

It's sloppy writing to switch person in the middle of copy. If you start with "SHE", don't suddenly talk "YOU" or "THEY".

Once you've established your YOU: male, female, teen-ager, suburbanite, antique lover, home sewer, etc., you'll find that your copy is easier to write because you can address yourself to that one person.

The quintessence of the YOU approach was a campaign Macy*s did some years ago. We realized that we were just too big for some people to shop in comfort. We ran a series of ads explaining (in terms of specific merchandise assortments) that, because we were a giant, we had something for everyone. Clearly not the same thing. Because "Macy*s has only one customer..you. Maybe that's why we have more customers than any other store."

Timeliness

This is a neat way of relating to your reader. You must be contemporary not just in language, but in ideas. If consumerism is on everybody's lips and in the headlines of your newspaper, then talk consumers. Ecology, education, computers, energy, Women's Lib. Whatever your customer's bag is. If there's a book of the moment or a hot TV series, play on the name. If cooking is the new sport in town, give it a nod in your copy. The last line of a fashion ad could be "And what better way to look when you've invited another couple to share your Veal Cordon Bleu?" It's a throw-away thing that makes your ad come to life.

It must be timely, but even here there are taboos. The original headline for the housewares ad quoted on page 27 was "In this kitchen, pot is a pan." We didn't dare. Marijuana and a family store!

When "The Graduate" was dinner table talk, our spice ad asked "Will it be parsley, sage, rosemary, or thyme?".... from one of its songs.

When everybody was concerned over status symbols, we said "Give him the status gift: a fur hat."

But when women were marching for equal rights, we said "Remember when fur hats were a gift only for women? This Christmas we give men equal rights." Notice the shift in emphasis.

Be Specific

The more specific the better. What does a woman learn about a chair if you say it's for any home? Or a dress for any occasion? (When my students use the phrase, I always ask..for swimming, too?)

If, heaven help us, your chair is, indeed, for any home, say so in specific language. "Whether you live with contemporary, traditional, or Colonial." Or, better yet, "Whether you live with Plexiglas, Queen Anne, or maple." If the dress is suitable for any occasion (except swimming) and that's about all you can say for it, then "It'll take you blithely from early a.m. to a late night-cap for two".

Most generalities are typewriter patter, mere filler that sells nothing, creates neither mood nor urgency.

As part of a campaign to attract young people, Macy*s opened its Housewares Show with an assortment of unusual pots. The copy was deliberately written in third person rather than second. See how it turns generalities into specifics.

"Here they go . . with their paellas, souffles, and shashliks. The generation that was raised on peanut butter and jelly. And copped out on the routine, the bland, the merely easy-to-cook. Who can tell a cardamon seed from a clove at 50 paces. Who can turn out an Indonesian sate or a Greek moussaka with equal skill. The generation to whom taste is an adventure of the senses, and cooking a creative experience. An who (male and female) are often more fascinated with the kitchen than their mothers.

Here goes Macy*s into the 70's ... with the professional gear that's making its way into even tiny kitchens. From French tart pans to Mongolian hot-pots. In aluminum, in enamel, in cast iron, in stainless steel, in copper, in glass, in earthenware .. non-stick and au naturel. An astonishment of pots and pans. From the obvious to the unexpected. Because the World's Largest Store just naturally has more .. of just about everything. For every generation.

Right now at Macy*s Housewares Show & Sale .. a mind-stretcher and a money-stretcher, too."

It could have been boiled down to "Young people today enjoy cooking, and we have pots for every purpose". But how dull.

Words That Work For You

A verb is worth a dozen adjectives. An off-beat noun, ditto. Look at these headlines from a promotion that got much of its distinction from the use of a vivid verb. Take the verbs away, and the headlines are flat.

"Revel in the collection of confections from Britain .. here and now".

"Love the many linens of Northern Ireland .. here and now".

"Collect the many antiques of Britain .. here and now".

"Behold the bounty of biscuits from Britain .. here and now".

"Savor the flavors of Britain .. here and now".

Verbs are action. They involve you. They make the reader want to do something.

> This is a trick you can train yourself to use. Write your copy, then examine it. Can I use a better word, a fresher word? Does this adjective add anything? Can I change my verb so I don't need the adjective, or maybe I can substitute an adverb?

How do you do it?

You write "a flattering shoe". You change it to "a shoe that flatters your foot outrageously."

You write "modern lamps". You change it to "contemporary lamps". Not much better. So you change it to "Lamps that reach into the future". Now you've started the reader's imagination going.

Or look what two words can do.

A paragraph in a Macy editorial ended "We're so proud of The Affordables at Macy*s that we've given each one a chrome-bright tag. Look for it when you shop." It didn't have quite the soaring lift we wanted, so it was changed. "Look for it when you shop.. and gloat!" A stopper, instead of a dying fall.

The Format and How to Keep It Fresh

You're stuck with a format. An ad every Thursday with a 56-character headline and 5 lines of copy.

Well, you can trim the layout with pretty words. Or you can make it work for you. Forget your format, and write the ad the way you think the merchandise requires it. Then rewrite it to the format. This is an elementary trick, but it keeps you from feeling like a prisoner. In short, don't think format. Think copy.

CHAPTER 7
THE DEMONS

Suddenly, customers have become consumers. With all the overtones the word has acquired. These days if you say kids' socks wear like iron and they only wear like cotton, the store can not only get expensive returns but maybe a lawsuit as well.

What's more, if an ad can possibly be interpreted to put down women or some ethnic group, you'll get stacks of letters. Maybe even enclosing torn charge cards.

It's unfortunate because, in the consumer's eye, we're being equated with used car dealers, TV repairmen, Madison Avenue manipulators, and other notorious double-talkers. Actually, most stores try hard to be honest. They've learned that honest ads are good ads. And the last thing in the world a store wants to do is offend any group of people. They're the store's most cherished asset: its customers.

Even being honest, by your own lights, is sometimes not enough these days. The FTC, the BB (Federal Trade Commission, Better Business Bureau) and other alphabetical agencies are watching over you.

Examine these facts:

1. The manufacturer says your special purchase of Jim-Jam overalls makes your price the lowest price in town.

2. Your information sheet on a knife sale says "Up to 50% less than manufacturer's list price".

3. You are having a drawing for a trip to the moon and you decide to call it Lunar Contest.

4. You've tried a face cream and it made your skin feel like a baby's.

5. You think Match-Mate would describe some pants and tops nicely.

6. The label on a pair of boots says "guaranteed waterproof".

7. Your buyer calls a blouse a silky blend of 45% acetate and 55% nylon.

You can use these facts in your ads, right? Wrong. If you're in New York, you can't use any of them, and in most cities you can't use most. Even if they're as accurate as Greenwich Observatory Time.

Why not? Because there are laws, regulations, newspaper censors, Better Business Bureaus, the FTC, and other things and groups to protect consumers, manufacturers, and your competition. But remember, they protect you, too. From unscrupulous competitors, from dishonest advertising by others.

Now, let's look at the "facts" one by one.

1. In New York, we can't say lowest price in town even if we can prove it. The newspapers do not permit competitive statements. We can't even make general statements about discount prices. We can only mention discount prices on specific merchandise.

2. You can't say "up to 50% off". You must give actual from-to percentages, and you'd better have a good quantity at that upper figure or your Better Business Bureau may breathe down your neck. And quoting manufacturer's list price is illegal in some areas.

3. In New York, we can't have a contest, only a drawing.

4. Pure Food and Drug regulations say that a cream doesn't make your skin young. It can feel as though it's younger, or seem to look younger.

5. Match-Mates is a registered trade mark. Use it otherwise and you'll be sued.

6. The FTC says you can't use the world "guaranteed" unless you spell out the guarantee. Will they replace the boots if they leak? Without charge?

7. You must name the fiber with the higher percentage first. Nor should you use adjectives like silky or lineny unless you're describing real silk or linen.

Does this hamstring you? No. You simply don't fight City Hall. You write it right the first time. You may think the laws are silly, and some of them are, but why re-do an ad at the last minute to prove your point? Instead, you arm yourself with weasel words that are legally correct but equivocal. Our newspapers in New York won't let us make competitive statements. O.K. We can't say "Biggest Sale this year". So we say "OUR Biggest Sale this year". Non-competitive, but mighty strong. You can't say "Where have you seen shirts for so little?" So you say "When have you seen shirts for so little?" Fun and games for all.

You must also be sure that your copy is consistent with store policy. It may be your store policy not to use comparative quotes. Or to include the phone number in every ad. Whatever it is, it's not yours to violate. Surprisingly, you sometimes end up with a better ad because you don't take the easy, obvious way out. You are forced to think the problem through. How can I imply that this coat looks like seal without using the word seal?

The other demon that haunts writers is the need to be sure. Is the manufacturer's literature fact or fancy? Is the buyer romanticizing? If your store has no way of checking, well, a large grain of salt helps. When superlatives are around, it's better to understate than to end up misleading your customers. Especially since you're the one who will have to answer the angry letters.

Naivete is a sign of the amateur. But be consoled. After you've been in the business a while, you will acquire a set of questions to ask, and sufficient background, to protect yourself and your readers.

CHAPTER 8
WATCH YOUR LANGUAGE

The language of an ad should be as close to conversation as possible . . only better.

How much better? Don't be so clever that people remember the ad, rather than *whose* ad. Don't be so clever that your words get in the way of selling goods.

Words acquire a flavor, an aura that has little to do with their dictionary meaning. Except for its violent implications, nothing could be more innocent than "bloody," yet it was such a dirty word in Victorian England that they described meat as "ensanguined".

Some words are plain old-fashioned. "You'll be beautifully clad". Not in the 2nd half of the 20th century, you won't! We grow up reading the literature of the past, so when we start writing, words that belong to the past pop into our minds and our prose. On the other hand, some words grow old-fashioned suddenly. One day "slacks" became "pants".

You can avoid old-fashioned words by reading your copy aloud. Any word that you would not use in conversation should be questioned. Occasionally, you will use an out-of-date or literary word deliberately. That's fine, if it's obvious that you're doing it deliberately. Often you will use an unusual word, but it should be unusual in the way or context in which you are using it. . . not in itself. For example, etcetera is a common word. Yet how unusual it is in this sentence: "All the little etceteras a worldly woman collects".

Words go through popularity cycles. For a while, every third ad will use "enchanting". Or "devastating". Then they seem to disappear. In the past 10 years advertising vocabulary has changed mightily. Stores have caught up with the fact that their customers are better educated than ever. So if you say "add a dollop of green", the buyer won't complain that nobody knows what dollop means.

Some words have unpleasant connotations. "Cheap" sounds shoddy, but "bargain" or "buy" has no quality implication.

Some words are just plain clunky and awkward. "See our merchandise". You don't shop for "merchandise". "Spark your Spring appearance" walks on heavy feet. "That necessary accessory" has an accidental assonance that's disturbing, as well as an unnecessary "that". The use of "that" for emphasis (for that important dinner, for that look of elegance) is poor writing, and not part of the pattern of normal speech.

Some words and phrases are so trite they're meaningless. Here are a few choice gems. A spring must. Brand new. In the fashion spotlight. Revolutionary discovery. Delicately trimmed. Perfect for your wardrobe. The most wanted colors. Touch of elegance.

And on and on and on.

Sometimes, however, the obvious word is the right word. The fashion word of the moment, no matter how often it's used, is irreproachable. And there are, as we have seen, timely this-minute words and phrases that can and should be used.

You must be careful to avoid phrases with hidden double meanings, or you'll hear from every little old lady for miles around. A cherished one was a sign in a store window: "The dress for all your affairs". There are more subtle innuendoes that are equally dangerous. A special purchase where you talked a manufacturer into cutting his prices may sound good to you, but the customer may react with...they put the screws on the poor guy.

Everyone who can pronounce the word "advertising" has heard that you shouldn't use negatives in copy, and will tell you. Forget it. Some of the most successful ads, slogans, and campaigns have been built on negatives. "Nobody but nobody undersells Gimbels", to cite just one.

How about sentence construction? The simpler the better. Preferably one idea to a sentence. If you find that you have written a long sentence, see if you can break it into two or even three parts.

Should you write complete or incomplete sentences? That depends on you. A series of short incomplete sentences results in a certain kind of beat that can be exciting. But don't do it if it doesn't come naturally. Henri Bendel in New York, for a while, was doing a series of single words. Each with a period at the end of it, like a sentence. Interesting when handled well, but tricky to do.

Some writers are fond of headlines that are questions. They feel that this captures the reader's attention more readily than a flat statement. A question intrigues. You want to know the answer so you keep on reading. It's an easy trick. Poets have been doing it for centuries.

All you do is take your headline and restate it in question form. "Our new piano center opens with a concert" becomes "How do we open our new piano center? With music, music, music!"

You may have heard that a question in a heading is dangerous; it can invite a negative answer. Nonsense. Only if you ask a silly question. Questions are a good technique to freshen tired prose.

Should you use bullet copy? Yes. When you're trying to be terse, factual, and the facts speak for tnemselves. Especially when you have a long list of specifications that must be included. A series of bullets breaks up the mass of verbiage. Bullets are not an ideal selling tool. They leave you no room for persuasion. But they have their place.

Punctuation? You may have no choice. Your store or your newspaper may dictate a style. The ideal is to punctuate for sense, to make your copy easy to read. (Which is what punctuation is all about.) Don't be afraid of semi-colons and colons. Don't load your copy with unnecessary commas. And never use commas or periods at the ends of lines in headings.

"Involvement, satisfaction, communication" is fine as one line. But see how dumb this looks:

> Involvement,
> satisfaction,
> communication.

Exclamation points? Only when you have an exclamation, an exhortation. The use of the exclamation point is too often a substitute for good copy. If you write it well, you don't need the exclamation point to add excitement.

Now let's see what a difference language and sentence structure can make. Copy B is a rewrite of copy A (by another writer). The facts in both versions are identical. The point of view is identical. The merchandise problem is identical. Even the headline is identical.

```
If you have a house, apartment, just a room, even
a pad . . read on:
```

COPY A

```
Hip or square, wait till you see what a fashion face-
lifting we've given the whole place. Are you with the
square majority? We've more Heritage than ever. New
Cameo bedroom and dining room groups, aristocratic as a
formal Italian villa, with exquisitely matched walnut
veneers and classic hardware, are placed in lovely vig-
nettes. Our magnificently done bedroom-sitting room
holds Heritage Madrigal and many upholstered designs.
And for the beautiful people, our just-opened Vendome
Gallery is a decorator's heaven.
Commodore, designed by us and made for us alone, is so
outstanding it gets a model room of its own. Inspired from
last century sea chests, the pecan finished bedroom is
brass bound. Teeny-boppers to go-go adults welcome the
versatile news in Young America bedrooms. A Pennsylvania
Dutch group in with colorful decals. On sale,
Directional's swinging new walnut finished group. Find
new and old ways to sleep. Trend Setter dual sleep furni-
```

ture almost furnishes a room. Simmons' firm twin or full mattress now at an old fashioned 39.95. Take home plenty of ideas from model rooms, fresh from creative hands. See a duplicate of the newly married's apartment found in January Bride's Magazine, bright with the talent of England's own Terence Conran. And more, more. Bell-bottom set, check out the imported and domestic modern. Foam, chrome and Plexiglas swirling, curving and comfortable; the sofa and chair pieces George Mulhouser did for Directional˙.
Tommorrrow, come, see everything.

COPY B

Tomorrow, see what can happen inside 4 walls... your walls. Furniture so new that this is its premiere. Decorating ideas in such abundance you could spend the week here. Rooms, vignettes, settings... by the scores. Our elegant new Vendome gallery, where every desk and table has a continental accent. New Commodore, lifted from old Royal Navy sea chests, designed by Macy*s and made just for us. A bedroom-sitting room, rich with the Spanish flavor of Heritage's Madrigal. The aristocratic Italian formality of new Cameo by Heritage. Even a duplicate of the apartment in January Bride's magazine, bright with the innovations of Terence Conran, whom we introduced to the U.S.A. All so this-moment that you may still find us with paint brushes in our hands and pins in our mouth tomorrow. For moderns: new art forms in foam and chrome and plastic. The simplicity of Directional... and the fantasies of George Mulhauser and Milo Baughman. For teenagers: would you believe Pennsylvania Dutch with decals? For everybody: more ways to make your bed and lie in it than you could dream of, from Trend Setter's clever are-they-or-aren't they sleepers, to an old-fashioned sale of Simmons mattresses for a mere 39.95. And more... the world's largest furniture floor full. Aisles of tables. Collections of chairs. Droves of dining rooms. Bevies of bedrooms. Many at sale-sale-sale prices. And we're wall-to-wall with ideas to set off your furniture, new ways to cover floors, hang pictures, stack books, drape windows, display bibelots. It's all new, all a joy to behold. Come enjoy it all. Come to Macy*s 9th floor. Tomorrow.

The difference between A and B? Night and day! B has urgency, immediacy. It doesn't rely on current slang like "hip or square" to pinpoint the audience. It talks benefits. It's fresh in its language (count the cliches in A). It has a pace, a lift that turns what's basically an inventory in A into excitement. In short, it sells.

CHAPTER 9

THE DO'S AND THE DON'TS

There are no irreversible rules to writing copy. However, there are a few do's and don'ts that will help you write better copy. Some of them are discussed at length in other parts of this book, but here in its briefest form is the copywriter's guide.

Don't use hyperbole. At Macy*s, there was a sign in every copywriter's office "Don't use superlatives; they lead to exaggeration". They also trip you. If you say this is our biggest sale, what do you do next week or next month or even next year when you have a bigger one?

Don't indulge in reached-for metaphors and similes. Once at Bamberger's, a copywriter had the usual crop of navy blue dresses for Easter. Her headline (which fortunately never got into print) was: "This year the Easter bunny will lay navy blue eggs."

Don't make bad puns. Good ones are O.K. Who's to decide if they're good? We have what we call a wince club. If anybody winces at a word, we reconsider it. Sometimes we're democratic and take a vote. There's no one best headline, no one best piece of copy. There are many ways to solve problems. Which, of course, does not mean that you shouldn't fight for something you think is right. Even a pun. But know when to give up.

Avoid cliches. They're like the picture on the wall that's been there for years. They make no impact. Unless you are using the cliches as a put on and having a bit of fun. Like a series based on cliches about wool. "Wolf in sheep's clothing" for a man's suit ad. "Pull the wool over your eyes" for sweaters, etc. But this was deliberate and included the reader in the joke of using the cliche as though it were fresh-minted.

Don't use foreign words. It may make you feel chic to say chapeau for hat, but it's old hat. There are plenty of good English words, and it's pretty weak copy that has to rely on French to make its point. Exception: if the word is in good current fashion usage, like "Blouson" is at this writing. Or it has become part of the English language. Like chic.

Don't be patronizing. Never preach or imply that you know more than the reader. You may be wrong. Every time a woman sees a camera ad that tells her this camera is easy enough for a woman to use, she probably boils.

Don't take advantage of poetic license. Leave it to the poets. If you're selling a $200 sofa, don't go on and on about how deep and puffy and luxurious it is. Your customer's reaction? If it's that good, why is it only $200? Something may be wrong. Or, if it's an item you're selling by mail, and your freedom with facts is persuasive enough to bring in the orders. . .wait till you see the number of returns you get.

Don't be technically sloppy. Nobody is going to pick up your errors in spelling, grammar, punctuation, or references. Except your readers. Say "like" when you should say "as" (unless you're a cigarette company) and you'll get a letter from every other English teacher. Check and doublecheck whenever you have the slightest doubt. I have quoted the headline on the golf ball that drove "further". I used it because, to my ear, it sounded further than farther. When the letters came in telling us that "farther" should be used for distance, I was prepared. I had the pleasure of smugly referring the writers to the dictionary. I had checked it myself and, according to Webster, "further" can also be used for distance.

Do be personal, warm, friendly. You're talking to everybody but, if I'm the reader, you're talking directly to me. That's why we always say you and your. Not THE home, but YOUR home. Not kitchen, but YOUR kitchen. Not THEY do, but YOU do. Exception: when your ad is other-directed. One of Macy's most interesting ads in 1970 was a bridal ad. It showed the bride in bridal gown, and the groom on a motorcycle. But we weren't talking to the bride and groom. We were talking to the parents who foot the bills for weddings. We were talking *about* the bride and groom and entered the minds of the readers by talking "them". So we said "There they go . . . into the 70's. The generation that threw out the rule book. Who opted for ideals instead of things. Who questioned values instead of accepting them. Who will soon be raising its own new generation." Then into the bridal bit, the bridal show, the works. It pulled large audiences, so we must have done something right.

Do talk woman-to-woman, man-to-man, adult-to-child, when it's appropriate. Take the reader into your confidence. "Aren't you glad slim shoes are back?" Try first person copy once in a while, if you can write it without being coy. In a year when striped shirts are selling, instead of "Give every man you know a striped shirt this Christmas", try "This year, I'm even giving my grandfather a striped shirt".

Do be enthusiastic, up-beat. Good copywriters want to buy almost everything they write about. The most optimistic prose in the world is copy. There are no duds, no mistakes, nothing to depress you. Maybe that's why advertising has gotten into the business of selling candidates to the public. To the copywriter, there are no warts.

Do be informative. A customer wants the facts. But be selective. If your art shows long sleeves, skip it, unless sleeves are the fashion news. Your customer wants to know fabric, size, construction details, all the little bugs that sound uncreative. . even the department and floor line and shipping charges. It makes it easier for her to shop. And, in home furnishings, she wants to know everything. Center-guided drawers may not sound like immortal prose, but it may make the sale for you.

Do use the fresh word, the unexpected word. Not "an assortment of wigs", but "a glory of wigs". Not "special" but "remarkable". Use the trick mentioned. Write your copy the way it comes naturally, then go over it, noun for noun, verb for verb, adjective for adjective to see if you can make it more vivid. Warning: don't use obscure words in your attempt to be different, or your copy will be heavy-handed. Glory, for example, is a perfectly familiar word, but used instead of assortment, it acquires newness. (And has lovely echoes of a woman's crowning glory when used for wigs.)

Do see goods from the customer's point of view. It doesn't matter whether you like it or not. If it fills a need, then it can be sold. It's your job to present the merchandise as desirable to the customer for whom it's intended. Maybe you wouldn't have a reclining chair as a gift, but lots of people want them. Forget your personal taste . . and let your enthusiasm take over.

Do use the simple declarative sentence, whenever possible. "We love blue this year". Not "Blue is loved by us this year". Be active not passive. Keep your sentences as simple as possible. If you lose a customer in the middle of a sentence, you'll never get her back into your ad.

Do always urge immediate action. The come see, come try, come buy idea. The don't miss it idea. Not necessarily in that language, of course, but always giving the feeling of immediacy. Urgency.

CHAPTER 10
THE VERSUS PROBLEM

Short Copy vs. Long

One side says: Write short copy. As short as you can without sacrificing your selling points or urge to action. Customers today have a lot of competition for their time. They don't want to wade through paragraphs of precious prose. If you can't bear to cut one priceless word, you're not being very professional.

The other side says: Write long copy, long enough to tell your whole story. Then stop. The reader will go on and on, if fascinated. Want to prove it to yourself? Make a mistake. Have a typographical error on line 28 or misquote Shakespeare, and you'll get 2 dozen letters. Whom do you believe? Both. Some ads can be written short, some must be long.

Let me explain, by example.

One of the shortest ads ever announced Macy*s 100th Anniversary. The page had an anniversary symbol and all it said was "Tomorrow a year of celebration begins. . . Macy*s 100th Anniversary." What else was there to say? There were a half dozen other ads in the paper with the events and the excitement. The brevity of this ad was dramatic.

One of the very longest was an ad on Macy*s Meat Department. The problem was: how do you explain quality? The ad let the facts speak for themselves. How the chicken you buy today was eating corn yesterday in Maine. How our packer looked over 1900 cattle to find 50 steer good enough for us. 4 pages of double-spaced typewritten copy! The ad pulled like crazy (they even had a run on calves liver) because this was the right way to sell the idea of quality . . . in this case. And it won a prize.

Fashion copy is usually short. Since the picture tells most of the story, all you do is add a little romance, give the fashion news and the facts. Usually. For as I write this, Altman's in New York has been doing long, long copy on fashion ads for about 3 years. Ads that have helped give Altman's a new fashion reputation, sold tons of goods, and been envied by anyone who's ever written a line of copy.

Why? Because these are *good* ads with *good* copy. Fascinating copy that comes out of the merchandise and talks to readers like peers.

Just remember: it's not the length of the copy that counts, but the quality. There have been plenty of great long ads, and plenty of 35 word duds.

Think your problem through before you decide whether your ad is to be short or long. Let the contents decide. Then go over it and take the fat out. It'll hurt, but you'll find that whole chunks can go.

Dramatize The Art vs. Dramative The Copy

One side says: If you don't have big dramatic art, readers will turn the page. They've got to see what you're selling.

The other side says: If you don't sell them and make them come in, what's the point of running the ad?

The decision? Let art tell the story, when it can do it effectively. A new fashion, whether it's ready-to-wear or hard goods. An astonishing assortment (showing 52 coffee pots is more convincing than saying you have 52 types of coffee pots). Proportioned lengths, whether they're curtains or pants. Patterns... on anything from silver to fabrics.

Let copy tell the story when you're selling what a thing does, rather than what it is. Paint, cosmetics, drip-dry, mattresses, and such. Or items like hosiery where one pair looks like the next.

Nobody ever bought a can of paint because he liked the way the can looked . . or because the picture showed Lincoln's doctor's dog painting the dog-house. Here, more than ever, make sure your language talks benefit rather than being a label. Instead of saying "Flat Wall Paint:", you'll attract the eye much faster if you say "Happiness is a yellow bedroom". This is true whenever you sell what a product does. Let the reader in on it immediately.

One Idea vs. Lots of Ideas

One side says: People are simple. They can only digest one idea at a time. Don't confuse them with a lot of ideas in a piece of copy.

The other side says: The more ideas you can throw at them, the more likely you are to sell the goods. Tell them about your assortment of similar items, how many ways they can use it, talk about your low price, how hard you worked to get it for them, how you stand behind it, and don't forget it makes a good gift, too. All in a snappy 6-word heading.

Well, neither side is right. Use one idea...at a time. Take your strongest selling point and make a heading out of it, in terms of the customer benefit. Then tell all the other stories. One by one. More than one idea in a sentence is just plain poor writing.

Consider the following piece of copy. The problem was an ad on wigs during the Christmas season, hopefully to be bought as gifts but also for the customer to buy for herself. We had to sell the gift idea, the wig idea, the assortment idea. We had to mention Adolfo. We had to say "all this and more for Christmas". Notice how each idea is kept separate, so there is no confusion; yet the ad hangs together. (Captions gave the details and prices.)

```
Every girl
deserves a
Christmas gift
...from herself
```

From you to you...a wig. The new indispensable. Especially now when you don't have a moment to do your hair. (Lucky you!) Come be tempted by our wigs by the happy hundreds. Wigs that pass-for-real and strictly-for-fun wigs. Even wigs by Adolfo. All pre-styled, washable, ready-to-wear. This minute. From you to you. Or for a jubilant friend this Christmas. All this and more, frivolously yours for Christmas.

Hard Sell vs. Soft Sell

Can you lure more people with loud noise or soft music? It depends...on what you're selling and how you do it. There is a school of thought that says you can take any product and bang away at it and you'll succeed in business. That's fine, if you have one product like Anacin. But if you're a store, with thousands of products, you may just give your customers a headache. There must be a proper balance.

First, let's define our terms.

Soft sell is indirect. It creates a desire to buy at some time. It lets the customer sell herself. It sells a mood, a flavor, a fashion, an image, an idea. These may be so irresistible that they stir the customer to immediate action, but the ad itself never pounds.

Hard sell is an exhortation. It says, in essence, that if you don't do something fast, you're a fool.

Most sale ads are, by their nature, hard sell. But there are always the exceptions. In a year when the stock market was dropping and unemployment rising, Macy*s Spring Sale booklet did not merely shout "Sale! Save! Big Buys!" No, it concentrated on what people were feeling and had a paragraph on the booklet cover that started "If you're getting careful about how you spend your money, consider Macy*s Spring Sale". Low key? Yes. Effective? Very, in terms of volume produced.

Hard sell, however, is not limited to sales. The threat ad is also hard sell. Do you have dandruff? Do you smell? TV is full of them. Discount advertising is hard sell even when the word sale isn't or can't be used.

"Buy your air conditioner now before temperatures soar" is hard sell. "Revolutionary new discovery" is hard sell.

In Greater New York, Alexander's consistently ran fashion advertising that was hard sell: fashion at a price. They used the word INCREDIBLE in giant type across a whole page, which gave it a hard sell look.

You can even write a hard sell ad for quality goods, spelling out its superiorities so the reader thinks that paying more will result in more value. Luxury automobiles have done it. Well.

Maybe those people who say you can be hard sell on any subject are right! But often a soft word is more productive.

CHAPTER 11
THE BIGGEST SALE EVER

Sale copy looks so easy to write. Trot out your superlatives, add a few exclamation points, make the type bigger, and you have a sale ad. Or do you? Not unless it has these three characteristics:
1. urgency
2. believability
3. simplicity

Urgency

The purpose of a sale ad is to move quantities of merchandise in a hurry. Your job is to move people into the store in a hurry.

How do you do it?

If your sale is for a limited time, use that fact prominently.

Today only! 3-day sale! Last day! Saturday only! 12 hour sale!

If time is not limited, there are other ways to add urgency, in headlines and body copy. Here are a few. You can take it from there.

A sale too important to miss
Sale starts at 9:30 tomorrow
Tomorrow you can save 43% on a new sofa

(Note: using "tomorrow" this way does not commit you to a one-day sale, but gives your ad some of the urgency.)

Come early for the best buys
Shop early, shop late, but don't pass up this sale
Every Spring coat sale-priced now
Only 130 coats at these sale prices. Now.

Limited quantities
First time at this price
Price goes back up tomorrow

The urgency, and the savings idea, should be carried through to the end of your copy. "Come see this unexpected buy in shoes on our umpteenth floor". "Why wait to have your floor covered when it costs so little now?" "Don't miss this chance to own a suede jacket for less than you expected to pay".

Believability

The most powerful sale advertising always gives the customer *a good reason for the sale*. It bridges the credibility gap. After all, they know you're not in business to give things away.

The reason can vary from Founder's Day to a warm winter to a manufacturer going out of business.

That's why so many stores concentrate their sales in specific periods of the year and use an "umbrella" for them, like Birthday Sale or Annual Spring Sale or Mid-Winter Clearance. These give a reason for a sale. (Beside which, the fewer sales you have, the more convincing they are. If you raise your voice only once in a while, people will listen.)

The "umbrella" can ride over a single event as well as a store-wide sale. January Coat Sale. White Sale. February Furniture Sale. Once-a-Year Sale of Discontinued Patterns. Any of these, and their many kind, creates instant communication, needs no explanation.

It is your job to dig out the reason, if any, for a sale. Often, unfortunately, it's only the need to meet last year's figures. Then you're on your own. If you can't give the customer a reason for the sale, at least provide a special reason for buying. There's usually at least some seasonal need you can hitch your sale ad to. "What a time for a china sale . . when you're expecting 15 for Thanksgiving Dinner". "A boot sale . . and still half the winter to go". But don't say "The sale you've been waiting for". Tell them why.

Use an idea, not a label. "Sale of Fans" is so-what. "A Sale of Fans now?" calls for a response.

If you don't have an umbrella, substitute an idea. It works. Sometimes you're lucky and you can have both. A few years ago, during Macy*s annual storewide sale, 15 items of better merchandise were combined on one page under the headline "The better things of life at beautiful sale prices". No illustrations. Each item became, basically, a powerful one-liner with a smaller line carrying the facts. Door-busters, but door-busters with a difference. For example:

Wouldn't you get more pleasure out of using a $50 tennis racket? Tomorrow $25.

Treasure-hunters! Lots of booty tomorrow in Macy*s Corner Shop. 20% to 50% off.

This is the kind of luggage you always wanted to arrive with. Now $49-$89.

The ad was so successful that it became an annual event.

Comparative quotes also help establish identifiable value. But the quotes must be believable (and honest). What's believable? If your merchandise is 75% less than last year's price, you may have a better ad if you bring it down to, say, 50%. Too big a quote might make it seem a dog you're stuck with. (You may have a little trouble convincing your merchants of this, but if you're a good salesman, you will.)

The strongest form a comparative quote can take is "yesterday's price", or "last week's price". It has immediacy. It says you marked it down right out of stock. It's convincing. Use it when you can legitimately. What if you can't use quotes? Then you imply them. "Can you imagine paying so little for." . . . . "Shop and compare. See what a buy this is." "A tremendous value at these prices."

Simplicity

A sale ad should be as close to a poster as possible, in graphics and in copy. Just enough copy to give the reason for the sale, communicate the value, and persuade the customer that only a fool would pass it up. This is no place for tricks of type, or fancy talk. Tell it like it is, and let it go.

P.S. on Fashion Sales

Fashion sale advertising differs from other sale ads since you must sell the fashion as well as the savings. Last year's pattern in towels (now discontinued) can see plenty of service, but who wants celluloid collars, even at a penny a throw?

You must use the fashion language you would use in a non-sale ad and, at the same time, make the customer feel she's a shrewd shopper if she buys at this price.

It's tempting to say "MINK SALE 999.99" and then do a straight fashion ad. Resist, or you'll have a weak ad. The savings idea must be integrated into headline and copy as well.

"Tomorrow the mink coat of your dreams at half price"
"If you've waited to buy mink, this sale is for you"

CHAPTER 12
THE IMAGE

What is a store's image? It's a combination of what people think of your store... and what you would like them to think of it.

Sometimes the image is simple. In New York, Alexander's is fashion at a price; Bergdorf's, fashion authority.

Sometimes the image is complex. If you are a large department store, like Macy*s or A & S, you have something for everyone. So you have many images, and often run 6 different campaigns simultaneously with 6 different image projections. It's perfectly possible for a department store to have a fashion image of one kind and a home furnishings image of another...and different customers for each.

A store's image should be reflected in its advertising, because this is how we show ourselves to our customers.

Advertising image can be the way an ad *looks* or what it *says*, or both. The personality of the ad. The thing that makes it possible for you to recognize a store's ad without looking at its logotype.

Every time you write an ad, you are reflecting and projecting an image. People believe what you say (or don't believe it, and that's an image of another kind). Your ideas and your language are part of the store's image. Terrifying, isn't it? Or maybe exhilarating.

But don't think this gives you license to make your store over... in words. Your copy must be written within the image of your store. Never forget: image starts with the merchandise and the management policy of the store. If you're a cheap john operation, for example, it's out of character to write ultra-sohpisticated or poetic prose. Why? Because a store cannot have two images... one in its advertising, another in the store.

If you give the impression in a robe ad that you are young and avant-garde, and customers rush in to find exactly 3 interesting robes in a welter of woolies and snuggies (with customers to match), they feel that they've been taken. Disaster lies this way.

It's equally disastrous to be without an image in advertising, or have a borrowed one. That kind of advertising is faceless and forgettable. It may be 20-20 hindsight, but most of the stores that have folded up in recent years had no clear and contemporary image.

Can you change the image of a store? Yes, but only if the store is better than its image in its advertising. Or vice versa. Or even in the process of up-grading itself.

Let me explain the vice-versa. It's no joke. When the now-legendary Bernice Fitzgibbon first came to Gimbels, it was almost shabby; badly-lit, old-fashioned. She made a virtue of it. "Plain old Gimbels has plain old-fashioned prices", and such. She was so successful in projecting a bargain image that the store prospered. The store was later beautifully remodeled and the next advertising generation had to change the old image.

Must you run a lot of major space institutionals to tell people what your store stands for? Not necessarily. In the New York area, Altman's, Saks Fifth Avenue, Bonwit Teller, among others, rarely run an institutional. Yet all you have to do is see their advertising to know what kind of stores they are. Their merchandise ads are a perfect mirror.

For years, Wallach's Men's Stores were consistently in the paper with very small but distinctive all-type ads that seemed, superficially, to be all chit-chat. But even now, men who say they never read ads know they can have a button sewn on at Wallach's, whether their suits were bought there or not.

Ohrbach's runs only a few ads a week in the New York Times. Some years ago, when they were doing a provocative campaign, a poll was taken to evaluate the advertising impression made on New York Times readers. One of the questions asked was: which stores run the most ads? Macy*s came first (correct). Then Ohrbach's. Actually, they're one of the smaller advertisers in New York, but their impact was so great, people thought Ohrbach's was always in the newspapers.

You don't really need institutional ads if your merchandise advertising tells your readers the kind of store you are. But a big institutional campaign is nice if you can afford it. Let's say you can. Where do you start? First you must ask yourself some questions.

What kind of people do I want to bring into my store who now don't shop here? Young or not so young, working women or women at home? Local customers or customers who come from a distance? Men? Families? A higher income group? A lower income group that's afraid to shop here? Target your audience.

What does my store have or do that my competition doesn't (or doesn't promote)? Charge account, extra shopping hours, parking space, free delivery, phone orders (or any other service from bridal register to custom-made sheets)? Assortment? Low prices? Range of prices, from low to high? Special shops? Designer names? Friendly sales people? Experienced sales people?

Match your store superiority and your audience, then develop your institutional idea. And prove it. Don't just boast idly.

There are few things less likely to be read and remembered than an ad which says your store is a fine store in general terms.

Be specific. Don't talk assortment. Show 32 handbags. Don't talk low price. Give examples of how low your prices are. Don't say you're easy to get to. Show a map and tell them how little gas they need to get to you. Spell out the routes, by car and public transportation. Don't say you have all the best names in furniture. List them.

Most of all, an institutional should be light-hearted. Not really funny, because humor so often misfires, but fun to read. Even when the subject is serious. Take credit. Grim, serious, touchy?

Macy*s pulled in thousands of coupons with an unconventional...and light-hearted...ad promoting charge accounts before Christmas. The advantages of having a Macy account were embodied in 10 characters, amusingly cartooned. Here's some of the copy:

HERE'S TO HARRIED HARRY-
HE HAS NO TIME TO TARRY
This year he's doing the Christmas shopping. We
un-harried him fast. We gave him equal rights: a
Macy account card in his own name, so he doesn't
have to use his wife's. Now he's setting records
for quick gift-gathering. Oh, happy happy Harry!

MEET DETERMINED DEBORAH
CHRISTMAS SHOPPING CAN'T STOP HER
She's set on buying all her gifts in a single day.
We wish her luck! And remind her that her Macy
account makes shopping faster. (You don't even
have to spell out your name and address... or
wait for change.)

INTRODUCING INDECISIVE IDA
THAT ETERNAL BACKSLIDER
She buys a gift today, changes her mind tomorrow.
But does she stand on refund lines? Not our Ida.
She flashes her Macy account card and signs. (One
thing she's never ambivalent about: carrying her
Macy card with her.)

... and 6 more, from statistical Steve to tied-down Taffy to bargain-hunting Bess to last-minute Lenore to peripatetic Pat to logical Lee.

The headline? It sat over a generously proportioned coupon at the bottom of the page in the form of a Christmas tree:

    and
   easier
   merrier
  more joyous
 Christmas shopping
with a Macy account
    to
    you
    too

Readers were, presumably, amused; they identified, and got the message. The coupons started pouring in.

Trick: If you can use an event, an occasion, or something of particular importance to your city as a jumping off point, you will have a more interesting institutional. Because it will be newsy. For example: St. Patrick's Day usually falls during Macy*s spring sale. When it does, Macy*s sometimes uses a St. Patrick's Day ad to urge people to see the Parade, then come shop at Macy*s. Subtly, of course. Cleverly, of course. Like the ad whose headline was "It's a great day to be hyphenated and happy" ... and continued:

"Mayor Lindsay recently pointed out a startling truth ... that, while New York is always called a melting pot, nothing has really melted. Blended a little, maybe, what with Chinese-Americans enjoying Jewish rye, and Scottish-Americans cheering Italian opera, and Afro-Americans living with Scandinavian furniture, and German-Americans collecting Mexican art, and so on. But each group that makes up our city is proud of its national origin, its hyphenated heritage. And, on St. Patrick's Day, all of us are glad ... for what would March 17th be without the Irish-Americans to parade so beguilingly on Fifth Avenue ... many of them three generations removed from the auld sod? For the St. Patrick's Day Parade is one of the exciting colorful things that make New York the exciting colorful city it is. That's why Macy*s hopes you enjoy the Parade, as marcher or spectator, then spend the rest of the day (and evening) at the store just about everybody shops, no matter where their grandfathers came from. Especially today, when we're in the midst of our huge all-store all-floor Spring sale, filled with the kind of thrifty Macy bargains that are our special 111 year tradition, inherited from <u>our</u> ancestor, Rowland H. Macy.

Macy*s and all New York wish you a fine St. Patrick's Day".

What if your budget doesn't run to full page institutionals? You can tell your story in top-of-the-page editorials. Since the space is small, the story should be simple and direct. The same message, with variations, should be repeated frequently.

For years and years, A & S ran a variation of this: a drawing of an Eskimo team. "A AMAALUS... UPAGASASIANGURUK NAAKITUINAAK*" was the headline. Then "*It's easy as Eskimo pie for the Polar population to voice this advice: 'A & S... it's worth a trip from anywhere.' "

The art and foreign language changed each time, and there was an alternate message... "Don't say you can't find it until you've tried A & S."

Simple, direct, amusing, sufficiently different to be interesting, and getting its message across clearly.

What if your budget doesn't even run to editorials? Then let your merchandise pages be your institutionals. They may prove to be the best institutionals of all. If you have an assortment story, let the merchandise and your headline (or your base line... surely you can afford a base line) tell it. Or a credit story. Or a price story. Or a service story. It's hard to think of a store message (with the possible exception of how you've been everybody's favorite store for 92 years) that can't be conveyed by the right choice of merchandise.

Sometimes you can steal a bit of space from the merchandise story. As Sears did in a powerful ad on children's sleepers before flame-retardants became suspect.

"Mary Ann Miller doesn't really care if her super sleepers are flame resistant

But her Mother does
And so does Sears"

Is it important to tell these stories? It certainly is, because this is what builds your image. It also polishes the lustre of an old image. A new generation of shoppers is constantly coming up. They don't know what your store stands for. You must tell them. Again and again and again.

What about slogans? It's a touchy subject because bosses love them. Unfortunately, slogans become a special sort of cliche. They're repeated so often they lose their impact. If you must have a slogan, change it from time to time. Explain it from time to time. Up-date it. Your store isn't the same store it was 50 years ago, why should you be using the same slogan? Also slogans tend to be self-serving and boastful. Which, as you should realize by now, advertising should not be.

CHAPTER 13
THE CAMPAIGN

A campaign is a series of ads...plus. Plus a theme, an idea, a point of view, a reason.

Must all ads in a campaign look and sound alike? No. If they look and sound too much alike, nobody will read ad #2-through-whatever. There must be certain elements, in graphics and copy, that strike a familiar recurrent note. That's all.

The ads must run at sufficiently frequent intervals so they have impact as a campaign. A concentrated effort.

They can be small ads or full pages. They can be storewide, for a department, for an event, for a sale, or as narrow as promoting a fashion or color. A campaign can be 6 ads or 60. It can be in newspapers, on radio, TV, in posters, windows, direct mail, and even match book covers. Or it can be just newspaper. Or just broadcast.

How does a campaign happen? It doesn't...usually. It's planned and prepared in advance of the normal advertising schedule. Or should be. It's a joint effort of merchants, copy, and art.

Let's suppose that you will have a new collection of fashions from Canada in October. There are 10 ads, each on a different classification of merchandise. How do you unify them into a campaign, tell your story, and sell the goods? You could say "Our new Canadian imports" across the top of each page, and let it go at that. A yawn and much too general.

Instead, examine the subject. Fashion from Canada is a surprise. News. So you develop a line. "From Canada, the new fashion frontier". That's better, but what does it do for the merchandise, for *me,* the customer?

You develop it further. "A collection of pants for you, from Canada...the new fashion frontier". Fine, except that it has no personality. No attention-getter.

This is where, as a writer, you make your contribution. You decide, instead of the trite "collection" to use a different unusual collective noun in each headline, preferably alliterative, because alliteration, well-handled, is in itself a stopper.

```
Now a pride of pants for you, from Canada ...
   the new fashion frontier
Now a blizzard of boots for you, from Canada ...
   the new fashion frontier
```

Do these headlines in themselves make a campaign? No, not any more than saying "No. 23 in a series of ads."

A prototype layout must be developed that will be repeated, with variations, for the whole campaign. Art and type decisions are made.

Then you follow through. You take your campaign idea and use it in some way in every block of copy. You can't just drop it.

Let's take the Canadian boot ad. Assume that you have 2 copy blocks and captions. Wouldn't it be a good idea to use one copy block for the merchandise, the other for the overall story?

Copy block #1

If you've never equated Canada with fashion, you're due for a surprise. Consider these boots. Suedes, krinkle leathers, buckles, bits, crepe soles, trapuntos . . every boot fashion you're looking for is here. Warmly lined, of course (after all, they're from Canada). Zipped, of course, and some with clever stretch tops. Superbly built, of course, on a slant toe last that's utter comfort. And we've saved the best surprise for the end . . the wonderful price, of course. Just $28 a pair. From Canada now . . waiting for you on Blank's 3rd floor.

Copy block #2

Come walk into our beautiful boots from Canada, and see all the other Canadian fashions we've collected for your winter. Fashions for men, from overcoats to suede coats to slacks to mukluks to fur hats. Fashions for children, from parkas to corduroys. Fashions for you, a profusion of pants coats and long coats and fake fur coats and sweaters and such. All of them proudly tagged to tell you that they're from Canada, the new fashion frontier. Come see them now at blah blah's . . . before the thermometer drops another five degrees.

Captions?

The high-heeled trapunto boot from Canada
. . . just $28.
The double-buckled boot from Canada
. . . just $28. Etc.

Copy block #1 would change with the merchandise. Copy block #2 would repeat in each ad with a different lead-in.

What we have done here with Canadian fashions can be done with any campaign.

1. *Tell the news, in newsy language.*

2. *Give your campaign a personality through language and art.*

3. *Be specific, not general.*

4. *Follow through, right to the floor line.*

That's a merchandise campaign. How about an idea campaign? the same principles apply. Whether it's as general as "the new woman" or as narrow as "today's kitchen floor."

There is an odd danger in a long extensive campaign. We get bored with it. We see every ad, so we assume our customers do. Then we want to change it. Resist. If it's a good campaign that's functioning well, keep it going. Tackle each ad as though it were a fresh ad, a completely new ad, as it may very well be to the reader.

Sometimes you can even run an almost identical ad, month after month. Macy*s discovered that, unless people are actually in the market for slip covers or rugs or some other major home items, they ignore the ads for these classifications. (Unlike fashion ads, or idea ads, which people read as news.) For 4 or 5 years, Macy*s ran what was basically the same slipcover ad. It asked "Do you need slipcovers?". The only variation was price, usually a sale, and description of fabrics. The ad pulled almost the identical number of responses every time, year after year.

That's getting mileage out of a campaign. There's another way to get good mileage: pick up elements of your campaign and use them in other ads. For example: the new now woman. The idea can be used, in a smaller way, in children's wear, men's wear (the husband of), home furnishings.

A bridal campaign can be extended to gifts, to the makings of a first home, fashions for honeymoons, your first dinner together.

A housewares campaign can include at-home and at-work-at-home fashions. Pots and pants. Copper and kaftans.

Elements of a service campaign can be used in a smaller way with appropriate merchandise. Shop at home with draperies. Monogramming with silver. Credit with a TV set.

The virtue of mileage is that, with the more recognition you get, the more effective your campaign.

But don't let the campaign beguile you. The ads within it still must be the best possible ads you can produce.

CHAPTER 14
CHRISTMAS COMES EVERY YEAR

So do the annual sales, the anniversaries, the holidays, the new shops or floors or stores.

These, in their way, are baby campaigns. Pre-planned, intensive, but limited in time.

The trouble is that they happen year after year after year.

The easy out is to say you're going to set a tradition and repeat the same ad or headline year after year after year.

Sometimes it works. A & S has been running the same Christmas ad for a long time: Merry Christmas in all the languages of the countries in the United Nations. It bears repetition because the message is timeless. Macy*s ad on its Thanksgiving Day Parade varies only in its facts, and it's been running since 1958. There are stores that have one sale a year, and they repeat the same ad announcing it.

Notice that all of these are institutional in nature. A once-a-year event. A single ad.

You cannot easily repeat a series of merchandise ads or even headlines because a) the merchandise changes b) the climate of buying and selling changes.

Let's look at some of the annual events that are perennial.

Christmas

On the hottest day in August, your boss may come to you and say "We need an idea for Christmas". Lucky you! Because August is not too early. If you do a catalogue or posters or direct mail, you're practically up to your deadline. The way Christmas is handled is a decision that will probably be made at a higher echelon, but the results affect your copy.

There are 3 basic ways to approach Christmas.

1. *Develop a line and use it on all your advertising,* letting the merchandise, by its nature, carry the gift message. "Woodies, the Christmas store". "Sears has everything for Christmas". "Christmas with Hahne's".

An interesting variation on this was Franklin Simon's one year. They had the line JOY. JOY. JOY. in a very large greyed type running across the page. Sometimes on top of the page, sometimes behind the merchandise. Almost subliminal in its message.

Your Christmas heading can be as general as Woodie's, or somewhat more specific, but still general. "More gift ideas from Joneses". "From our four floors of Christmas ideas". "The right gifts . . . at the right prices". If you expect to use the same headline over everything, it can't be too specific. It must fit everything. Often, this is the only kind you can use if your Christmas pages are all omnibus pages that include everything from carving sets to slippers.

2. *You can handle each ad individually,* working the Christmas gift idea into the headline in the way that best suits the merchandise. This may make for interesting ads, but it often loses impact. The campaign continuity is lost.

3. *You can take a large chunk of your Christmas advertising and decide in advance to make a campaign out of it.* (Other ads are treated individually.) You start with your store's major Christmas story. Then you translate it and give it personality. The story might be assortment. Convenience. Price. Originality. Brand names.

Let's assume that your story is your abundance of national brands. If your competition has only a scattering of famous names, this is a potential power-house at Christmas.

You sit down with merchants and collect the names. Then develop a theme.

This Christmas, give him Arrow, the name he knows and loves.

This Christmas, give her Van Raalte, the name she knows and loves.

The story is right, but it's dull. It's dull because you're reiterating the obvious. If Arrow, etc. are so famous, you don't need "the name he knows and loves". It's dull because you're not selling the merchandise.

You'd have a better campaign if you'd let the merchandise dictate your headline and use your famous brands as a secondary idea. Importantly.

Give them a flower garden this Christmas: Vera tablecloths
One of the many, many famous names you always find at Joneses

Van Raalte robes. . . for the woman you watch the Late Show with
One of the many, many famous names you always find at Joneses

The famous name idea could also be turned into a good continuing base line:

One of the many, many famous names for Christmas at Joneses

At Macy*s, Christmas campaigns are built on the assortment idea, this being Macy*s strength. No two years have been the same. Nor any two ads. They have often differed within the campaign in typography. But the layouts were variations on a theme, the artwork had the same personality, ad after ad.

The copy is something else. It's as far from formula as possible. One Christmas, for example, the assortment idea was developed in either a short editorial or a sub-head. The headlines? Like these:

Doesn't every girl want a handsome six-footer for

Christmas? (scarves)

If he's the man we think he is, you'll find his gift right here (wide belts)

Gifts to bring out their hidden talents (needlework)

Wouldn't you like to admire his legs for a change? (short komonos)

Some were in verse, like this one which produced a sell-out:

Even if they don't know a Rhone from a Rhine
They'll be flattered by your gift of wine

While your headline should spring from the merchandise, the headline or subhead should say "give", "gift", "Christmas" or something that says this is for Christmas-gift-giving.

Annual Sales and Anniversaries

We have discussed sale ads in Chapter 11, but there's a special point to remember about annual sales. Most stores run them about the same time. January White Sale, February Furniture Sale, August Fur Sale, January Coat Sale. Most stores arbitrarily have their birthday sales in October because this is good timing for a storewide sale. Many also have a big spring sale to inaugurate (and capitalize on) the change of season.

That means you and your competition will be running the same kinds of sales at roughly the same time.

You can bring more people into your store, if your sale sounds more exciting than the next guy's. And you can make it sound more exciting by adding an extra dimension.

As illustration, here are headlines from a Macy Spring Sale. It was a storewide event, so rather than talk merchandise, it built urgency in a very human way. Notice how the adjective changes. Subtle. (These were all 2 facing pages . . . double trucks.)

Call your mother-in-law to come baby-sit tomorrow
 . . because something exciting is happening tomorrow
MACY✻S SPRING SALE STARTS TOMORROW

Cook a casserole tonight for tomorrow's dinner
 .. because something exceptional is happening tomorrow
MACY*S SPRING SALE STARTS TOMORROW

Change your dentist appointment for later this week
 .. because something tremendous is happening tomorrow

Tell your boss you're taking a long lunch hour tomorrow
 .. because something unique is happening tomorrow

Turn off the TV set tonight right after the news
 .. because something thrifty is happening tomorrow

These are more than stoppers. Each heading represents a market: the suburban housewife, the working woman, and so on.

Using the same "happening" idea, see how differently it could get translated when there is a specific merchandise story...a White Sale.

LOOK WHAT'S HAPPENING IN BLANK'S
 WHITE SALE
A brilliance of colors in towels, a parade of patterns, solids, jacquards, reversibles. . . and even whites!

More coordinates for bed and bath. . . one modern look in more colors, more prints, more no-irons. and more.
THAT'S WHAT'S HAPPENING IN BLANK'S WHITE SALE

Certainly sounds like a lot more going on than "January White Sale", doesn't it?

As for anniversary sales, nobody cares whether you're 73 or 74. It's what you're doing for me today that counts. However, the round numbers... 25, 50, 100... can become meaningful handles if they carry events as well as sales. If your anniversary sale is your biggest sale of the year, this is a strong argument for shopping now. Use it.

OUR BIGGEST SALE OF THE YEAR
Joneses 73rd birthday sale

Trick: If it isn't your biggest, or you're afraid to go out on a limb, you can still make it sound special.

IT HAPPENS ONLY ONCE A YEAR! NOW.
Joneses Anniversary Sale

A sale this exciting comes only once a year!
JONESES ANNIVERSARY SALE

Try to persuade your art department to skip the birthday cake in the ad. It's trite, dull, and you don't need it. You'd be better off, for example, with a series of pictures of scenes from your town the year your store opened. Or quaint merchandise from that era, depending on how old you are. If you can't get photos (usually from your newspaper), interesting drawings would do. And that's just one of literally hundreds of ways to go. Including strong all-type. All a lot more effective than the cake and candles.

The New Stores, Floors, Shops

It is a waste of good money and good space to run an ad which says, in essence "You are cordially invited to see our new housewares department". It lacks drama. It lacks an impelling reason to come see. Instead, either dramatize the merchandise the customer can buy, or make an event out of your opening. Or both.

Come taste coffee brewed in an expresso pot
Learn how to wax your floors in less time
See 21 different kinds of carving knives
Collect a collection of mugs, all sale-priced
Watch the new fat-less fryer in action
Discover more baking pans than you can imagine
Browse through new imaginative gadgets
ALL THIS AND MORE WHEN OUR
NEW HOUSEWARES DEPARTMENT
OPENS TOMORROW

Do you see what that does? It talks customer benefit. It talks what *we're* doing for *you*. It's specific. It gives a reason for coming to your store. It sells.

CHAPTER 15
THE OTHER STORES

The broad general principles that make for good copy apply to all retail stores, not just department stores. However, some types of stores present special problems.

The Discount Store

They've upgraded their perception of themselves by calling themselves mass merchandisers. If it makes them happy, why not?

Whatever you call yourself, your major customer benefit is more for the dollar. Never forget it, or let your reader forget it.

In a sense, all the merchandise is always sale-priced at a discount store. Which means that all your advertising is basically sale advertising. Simple, direct, emphasizing value.

But price is not the only story. If you're advertising a national brand, give the brand name a big play. A national brand not only sounds trustworthy (they wouldn't be that famous if they weren't good, says Mrs. Consumer to herself), but is also identifiable value.

Remember, too, that there are customer benefits inherent in the merchandise. Explain them, and your value story grows stronger. Panty hose at 79¢ a pair is a bargain. Run-resistant panty hose in beige, bone, black, brown, and gray; in petite, average, and tall is an even bigger bargain. Be as specific as you can.

What if your store doesn't have enough depth of stock to advertise individual items, but promotes categories? There are 2 different ways to handle this.

1. *Don't generalize,* but treat the category as though it were a series of items. Which it is.

Tomorrow! 400 bathing suits at 9.99. 382 bathing suits at 10.99. 198 bathing suits at 12.99. One piece, two-piece, bikinis, dressmaker suits; cottons, stretch nylons, even expensive lycras. Pastels, dark colors, wild prints. For misses, for juniors, and some half-sizes for women.

Notice: not "wanted colors", but groups of colors; not "every style", but the styles spelled out. This technique can be used for everything from rugs to fur coats.

2. *Be specific about one item,* and use it as a symbol.

Tomorrow. . a 19.99 bathing suit for only 10.99! We have just 32 of these dressmaker cottons in a vivid Hawaiian print, so come early. And see our tremendous collection of other bathing suits at equally wonderful prices. Stretch nylon bikinis at just 9.99. Expensive Lycra one-piece slinks at 12.99. (and so forth)

Trick: If your store has negative qualities, turn them into advantages when you can. For example the bathing suit ad could end:

Don't expect carpeted dressing rooms. Wouldn't you rather have our give-away prices?

or

Come and carry your bathing suit home. No built-in delivery costs at Blah Blah ... that's one reason you pay so little.

Sure, they know this. But it's good to remind them.

There is a real temptation when your store has a genuine more-for-the-money every-day-of-the-year story to try to create either a resounding slogan or an institutional ad that tells people about it. Don't. The best way to convey a value story is with examples... with merchandise.

What does a discount store do when it has a sale? A sticky problem since, in theory at least, its prices are always lower than those of a conventional store.

How do you get across the idea that these prices are now lower than low? By saying precisely that. In the comparative: "Sale 1.99, our regular low price 2.49". In headings: "An even better buy now during our sale". "Always low-priced, now a remarkable bargain." Etc.

Branch Stores

Branch stores are profitable because they have a lower overhead, since they share certain things with the main store. Like buyers, credit department, advertising, top brass. To the copywriter, they present two kinds of problems.

1. Often the media — print and broadcast — that the main store uses does not reach the branch, or only in a small way. That means separate ads must be done, usually by the main store's advertising department. Often by people who have never seen the branch, and know nothing about the neighborhood it's in, or its customers.

If you write copy for a branch, get out there, even if it's on your own time. Talk to the store manager. Look at the homes in the area. Explore the shopping competition. See what people wear, what kind of cars they own. And read the local newspaper. Why? Because it's as important to know your audience as your merchandise.

2. If you use the same media for main store and branches, the problem may reach your desk only intermittently. Basically it's a merchandising dilemma. You have 6 handbags. The two most

interesting ones are only at the main store. The other four are at all other stores, except one store which has only three.

Do you run only the three bags that are at all stores? Or do you run six? If you run six, how do you handle the location line. (That's where you come in.)

You can say: "bags #1 and #2 at Jones Main Store; all others at Jones Zip, Hip, Pip, and Tip as well (except no #3 at Hip)."

Or you can hedge. You can say: "Street Floor, Jones Main Store and an assortment at Zip, Pip, Hip and Tip Shopping Plazas".

The latter may be more indirect, but it's less confusing to the customer. (If she will only settle for bag #1 and shops Hip Plaza, Hip will get it for her if your merchants are what they ought to be.) And you can dress it up by ringing variations on the word "assortment". An interesting array. A beautiful bag-full. A characteristic collection.

An institutional ad is something else. You would probably have to dilute it to skim milk if you wanted to include all stores.

Let me give you some simple examples.

You have 23 model rooms at your main store, and anywhere from 5 to 10 at each of your other stores.

Write your ad about the 23 rooms, and tell your readers you have model rooms in their neighborhood, too...not as many, but equally interesting.

You are introducing 24-hour phone service only at your main store. Write your ad completely on this new service. Then add a paragraph on the phone hours at your other stores.

Specialty Shops

The special problem of the specialty shop is personality. More than any other advertising, this advertising must have individuality and character.

It can be done with graphics: distinctive and consistent type and layout and art. But the best way is a combination of graphics and copy. Establish your audience and talk to them. Exaggerate your style. And always be personal. If your style is chit-chat, be gabby. If your style is terse, be laconic. . . .almost cryptic.

Look at the difference between these two versions of a small ad for a quilted robe. (The audience should be obvious to you.)

The Sunday robe. For your day away from it all. To be prettier in. A gathering of tiny roses. Quilted. Machine-washable nylon. White, pink, or blue. 10-16. $29.

Isn't Sunday wonderful? The one day you can have your second cup of coffee in a cup instead of a container. We hope you have a robe like this to match your mood. It's a relaxed puff of quilting, simply espaliered with tiny roses. Can't you just see yourself in it? Your bonus: for all its air of delicacy, it sails through the washing machine. White, pink, or blue nylon in sizes 10 to 16. $29.

If you'd like to know all about specialty store advertising (from copy to planning, from graphics to measuring results), see *"The Specialty Store and its Advertising"* Ocko and Rosenblum. Also published by the NRMA.

CHAPTER 16
MEET THE PRESS

Big stores have public relations departments. Small stores usually don't. As a result, they rarely do any p.r. But when they do, either the boss takes over or asks a copywriter to help. This can involve anything from writing a few bon mots he can toss off at the Elk's meeting to doing a story for the paper on a new product or event.

Sometimes the line between public relations and advertising is very thin but there is one fundamental difference. The store pays for its ads. Publicity is free, in theory at least. (There's a certain amount of quid pro quo: you're more likely to get publicity in the media you buy ads in.)

The great value of publicity is that, to readers, it's usually more convincing. They believe that if the newspapers say it's so, it must be so.

The Press Release

This is the main vehicle a store uses to get its stories into the paper, a magazine, or on the radio or TV.

A press release is very simple to write. In fact, you probably learned how to write it in composition class years ago. The important thing to remember is that a press release is *not* an ad. It's a news story with certain characteristics.

1. A press release must give the who, what, why, where, and when. Preferably in the first paragraph. Just as though you were a reporter reporting on an event.

2. It should include a quote: from the boss, the manager of a department, or shop, or even a customer whose opinion you have solicited.

3. Unlike an ad, a press release should be impersonal. There is no "you". Only an audience. Study the style of your newspaper.

4. It must be factual, with as few qualifying adjectives as possible. No hype. It should be written in complete sentences.

5. A press release should have a dateline; the earliest date you'd like to see it appear. That's usually a day or two before your own ad, if you're running one, breaks in the paper. Once you've advertised it, the newspaper no longer considers it news. You can prepare and send out your release in advance, but the top of your sheet should say "For release: (date)". Of course, if you want it in the paper immediately, it's "For immediate release".

Let's assume you work for Jones & Jones, a women's specialty store. They've just remodeled their better dress department, called "The Treasure House", and moved it to the Main Street side of the store. Here's the release you might write.

```
                           For release: April 6.

Tomorrow Jones & Jones will open its remodeled
Treasure House department which has been moved to
the Main Street side of the store. The designer
fashions featured in the Treasure House will now be
shown in a setting of pink brocaded walls and pale
woods, dominated by a large crystal chandelier from
Austria. Six new mirrored dressing rooms are cur-
tained in striped satin and have Louis XIV style
armchairs.

Mr. John Jones, whose family has been operating the
store on the corner of Main and Arbor Streets since
1942, said "We believe downtown City will remain
the preferred shopping area for most women. Our in-
vestment in remodeling Treasure House is proof of
this faith."
```

Opening day events will include informal modeling of new Spring fashions and personal appearances by designers Blah Blah and Blah Blah as well an orchid flown in from Hawaii for each customer.

Betty Brown, recently arrived from Big Burg, is the new buyer for Treasure House. Mary Smith, Laura Lady, and Sally Sunday, all residents of City, will continue their many years' service as Treasure House sales people.

Don't be upset if the newspaper rewrites your release. It's their job. Or if they don't run it at all. There's a lot of competition for that newspaper space. The more newsworthy your item, the more likely it is to appear. A new department would probably rate space; a cosmetics demonstration might not.

Whenever possible, a press release should include a picture, preferably an action shot with a person or persons in it. For example, the picture with the press release above could be a long shot of the new department with a model in the foreground. The caption: "Halston evening gown, one of the fashions to be modeled tomorrow in the Treasure House at Jones & Jones". An alternative would be a picture of the 3 sales people in the new department.

Hint: If you work for a small store, keep an eye open for events with public relations potential. Then suggest that you send a release to the media on the subject. As I said, most stores simply don't bother, yet this publicity is invaluable. It's a sure way to get to be teacher's pet.

Note on special event copy

The purpose of a special event is to build traffic. No matter how small it is. Otherwise it's not worth the bother. And the only way to build this traffic is by dramatizing the event.

If you bury your fashion show invitation or your cooking demonstration in the middle of your ad or at the bottom, a large potential audience is lost. All those people who don't normally read your ads.

If the special event is tied into the merchandise in your ad... a cosmetic clinic, for example... great. Build your ad around the clinic. Headline it. Then go into the merchandise story.

If the event is not related to your ad, take a box in a prominent place, preferably at the top of your ad, and talk about it.

In either case, make it sound exciting, make it sound urgent, make it sound big. Then watch them knock down the doors.

CHAPTER 17

YOU AND THE ART DEPARTMENT

It is a cliche in our business that the copy and art departments are always battling. Don't believe it! Some of the best ads come from discussions (not battles) between copy and art, particularly layout designers.

The job of the layout artist is to take all the elements of an ad... art, copy, type...and design a page that will attract and sell people. Just as your copy does. (It is the layout artist who usually selects the type.) You want emphasis for a phrase? It can be laid out so it's unmissable. You have a large wad of copy? It can be broken into segments, designed so it looks like less. You want a paragraph to stand out? It can be set in a different or bolder type face.

An example of how copy and art people together can create a better ad is a page I did on Macy*s York House Scotch. I thought readers would be fascinated, as I was, by the full story. I ended up with two pages of copy. I tried a shorter version. It wasn't as convincing... nor as interesting. Morris L. Rosenblum, then Macy*s Creative Director, has an art background. He looked at my copy and said ... maybe we can help you. He roughed a layout that showed 4 rows of 6 shot glasses each, brimming with Scotch. It said "liquor" right away. I then broke my copy into 24 paragraphs. Suddenly, instead of a page of type ... we had an ad.

As a writer, there are some layout principles you ought to know that will make it easier for you to work with the art department.

1. *A page must have a focal point.* A big illustration. Or a few big words. Where all things are equal, nothing is anything.

2. *Art and copy can't be half-and-half.* One or the other must be emphasized, dramatized. Or your ad is weak.

3. *Type is a gray mass,* from the designer's point of view. Lots of little gray masses make an ad spotty. A large gray mass makes it dull.

4. *Four or five different sizes and kinds of type* in an ad are poor design. They distract the reader.

5. *A word or short phrase sitting on a line by itself* at the end of a block of copy (we call it a "widow") is also distracting. And it looks sloppy...as if you didn't care.

6. *An ad needs some white space.* You can't cram it wall-to-wall with copy or art. (There are exceptions to this, but it's a good general principle.)

7. *You cannot have 6 (or 5 or 8) items on a page* and expect each one to take a different amount of space. It is bad scheduling...and, if the layout artist tried to design the page by slide rule, it's a mess. A page must have balance and symmetry of some sort.

From the writer's point of view, there are a few things a layout designer should understand...and you should watch for.

1. *Legibility.* There's no point writing a persuasive ad if it can't be read. It's better to cut your copy, if necessary, than have it set in such small type that only those with perfect vision can read it in a strong light. Too much big type is equally hard to read... really big...unless it has lots of air around it. The same is true of more than a few lines of italic.

2. *Emphasis.* The layout artist is concerned with design, not sense. Some don't even read the copy (good ones do). Nor does the layout artist usually know the merchandise story as well as you do. It's up to you to spell out what's important and what's less important. Before the layout is made.

3. *The eye can't read a single thought as a single thought* if it's in two drastically different sizes of type. If your headline is "Isn't this a wonderful time to save on boots?", it may get designed as

```
      Isn't this a wonderful time to
            SAVE ON BOOTS?
```

If that's the only way it will lay out, rewrite it as two separate thoughts:

> Isn't this a wonderful time to save?
> SALE OF BOOTS

4. *The immovable object: the format.* In other words, a pre-planned, pre-designed ad that you write copy to fit. Well, sometimes you *can* vary it.

Just as it's not always good business to merchandise to a format if it may result in less volume, there are times when copy really won't work within the format. If you have the right kind of relationship with your art department, you'd be surprised how many variations are possible. After all, you are both working for the same store, both want the best possible ad in the paper.

You usually have little to say in the matter of photography vs. art work. It's a store policy whether merchandise is photographed or drawn. If you have the option, you will choose the technique that suits the merchandise and your ad.

Which comes first... the layout or the copy?

In most stores, it is the copywriter who goes to meetings, who talks to buyers, who gets the information sheets, who handles the merchandise. Therefore, it makes sense to have the copy written first, then laid out. But not always. When a campaign is being planned, or a graphic style being established, it may come from the art department.

Because of the complexity of designing a catalogue or a booklet, this is usually designed first and the copywriter fits copy to the layout. When you have 10 or 12 items on a page, the copy is indeed a series of small gray masses, and the more symmetrical they are, the cleaner the page looks, the easier it is to read.

Some stores have a style that depends on a magnificent piece of art. Here, too, the layout is built around the art and done before the copy is written.

There is an art to working with the art department. Mostly it's the kind of approach that makes for good personal relationships in any situation. If you think they're trying to hog the space with pictures, don't tell them that. Explain the importance of the copy story. Don't you be a hog either. Remember there are times when the art *is* more important. Make layout suggestions, if you have them, but don't be upset if they're not used. Just as you know what makes better copy, they know what makes better design.

Try to sit down to discuss important ads with the designer. Kick ideas around. You'll both benefit. And you'll end up with much better ads.

Never but never storm in to tell the designer a layout is dreadful. It may be, but start by saying something nice about it. "This is very dramatic. I love your puppies in a basket. But..."

As I said, as a copywriter, you know more about the merchandise, the purpose of the ad, the whole picture. You probably know more about the store and its customers as well. Share that knowledge. Historically, the art department has worked in a vacuum. Making pretty pictures. Break the vacuum and you'll be amazed at the response. The cooperation.

Oh yes, one more thing. Have lunch with them and find out **their** gripes. In other words, be friends.

Note: Next time you're told a picture is worth a thousand words, point out that this maxim was invented thousands of years ago. When 99% of the public was illiterate! They couldn't read so, of course, a picture was worth a thousand words.

CHAPTER 18

RADIO: LEND US YOUR EARS

Anyone who can write an effective print ad can turn out an equally effective radio or TV commercial. Only the technique is different. And your radio station can almost always tell you whom you're talking to. Broadcast polarizes its audiences. Only young people tune into Station A... and long hairs of the other kind are the audience of Station B. A newspaper, on the other hand, may have one audience for its sports section, another for its editorials, and still another for its women's page.

How does a radio ad differ from a newspaper ad, and how do you handle it?

1. There is no stopper, no big headline or art. *You must get the listener's attention with words.*

2. The ear is less attentive than the eye. Reading takes full concentration, but you can listen with half an ear. That's why you must *repeat, repeat, repeat.*

3. Listeners can't go back to figure out what you mean. So keep your *sentences simple, brief, uncomplicated.*

4. There's no logotype to identify your store. Don't leave them wondering where they can get it. *Tell them again and again.*

5. You have no picture to support your prose. If there are important facts, *you must give word pictures.*

6. Words that look right don't always sound right, and some combinations or words make for stumbling. *Read your commercials out loud.*

7. *Your audience can't absorb and remember a lot of numbers.*

Don't try to give 3 prices, a phone number, and an extension in 30 seconds.

8. The announcer is not a spokesman for the store, but a third party. When he talks about your store, it's "they", not "we".

9. You have only one chance to *attract an audience. . with your lead-in.* If you don't catch them then, they'll turn off their ears.

Time on radio is usually sold as 10 second spots (also called IDs or identifications), 30 seconds, and full minutes.

You can get about 30 words in an ID, 75 words in 30 seconds, and 150 in a minute. Depending on your words. A polysyllabic message takes longer than one composed of one or two syllable words. A stop watch makes timing easy. If you don't try to kid yourself by reading too fast.

Many retail commercials are "live", read by a station announcer, for the simple reason that this eliminates production cost. It also gives you flexibility. You can have one commercial in the a.m., another in the p.m., or a dozen different ones during a single day. At no extra production cost.

How to Translate an Ad into a Commercial

No matter how great a newspaper ad is, you can't hand it to an announcer and say...here's my commercial. You must rewrite it for the air.

Filling in significant details that your pictures show.

Repeating the most important facts as often as possible.

Repeating your store name as often as you can gracefully.

Writing to a tempo that's for the ear rather than the eye.

Let me show you how it works, with an extreme example because this ad had miles of copy. Many chapters back, the very successful Macy golf ball ad was mentioned. Here is part of the copy.

We don't know
exactly why, but
this new
golf ball drives
4 yds. to 12 yds.
    further...
every time

Macy*s new XP/270, developed by MacGregor, tested and enthusiastically approved by Macy*s Bureau of Standards

Even the head of Macy*s Bureau of Standards (a dedicated golfer as well as an expert on the whys and wherefores of things) is happily astonished by the way this ball performs. It was tested against 5 of the best-known top quality balls, including 3 pro shop balls. Invariably, it went from 4 yards to 12 yards further when hit with a driver.

It passed the best test of all: the human test. (a paragraph on this)
Why does this ball drive further? (another paragraph)
What does the XP/270 mean to you? (still another paragraph)

Plus price, coupon, first and only at Macy*s, where to buy it, etc. A lot of stuff.

Here's how it was turned into a 30 second radio commercial for Father's Day (which added another character to the plot).

What better gift for your father... a golf ball that drives 4 yards to 12 yards further... every time. It's Macy*s new XP two-seventy golf ball. Tested by Macy*s Bureau of Standards. In the lab. On the golf course. Ball after ball, drive after drive, it traveled 4 yards to 12 yards further. Macy*s XP two-seventy golf ball, developed by MacGregor. Bound to make your father a happier golfer. Ten dollars the dozen. At Macy*s now for Father's Day. Amazing.

Notice how the most important facts are repeated: the gift for father idea, that it drives 4 to 12 yards further every time, that it's new, and the name of the ball. There are 4 "Macy*s" in the 30 seconds. And 3 other significant points: tested by Macy*s Bureau of Standards, the price, and the MacGregor name.

Notice that the customer benefits come first and get emphasis.

Notice that it's broken into short, speakable units. With time for the announcer to breathe.

Notice the up-beat ending. The unexpected word "amazing" that gives the commercial a personality.

Now let's see how this turns into a 10-second ID... with fewer facts, but the same personality.

What better gift for your father... a golf ball that drives 4 yards to 12 yards further... every time. Macy*s new XP two-seventy golf ball, tested by Macy*s. Amazing.

Sometimes you must walk away from the ad or campaign you're trying to translate because it won't work as radio.

After opening a new store in Brooklyn, Macy*s ran an extensive newspaper campaign, based on merchandise. Radio was confined to 10-second IDs. It was not possible to build the radio campaign on the ads. Instead, it concentrated on the news... the new Macy*s, its location, store hours. With spots like this:

What. . you haven't seen Macy*s KingsPlaza yet? Why are you waiting? Open till nine-thirty every night. Macy's new Kings Plaza. . .Flatbush Avenue and Avenue U in Brooklyn. What a store!

The Radio Commercial from Scratch

You handle this like any other ad. Collect your facts. Look at the merchandise. Find out the most important selling points. Establish your audience. Think it through. Then go, using the radio technique described.

Unlike a newspaper ad, where an indirect lead-in turns people off, on radio it turns them on. You must stop them before they start to absorb your message. (Sale commercials are different. See below.)

Your lead-in must intrigue. Talk news or customer benefits or relate to what customers have on their minds. Always in conversational language.

Here are some lead-ins from a Macy campaign. They were all 1 minute, all home-furnishings, non-sale. The pitch was Macy*s depth of assortment. They ran on New York's two fine music stations which have a literate, sophisticated audience.

Do you have a floor to cover? Then listen carefully. Macy*s has only one minute to give you some good advice.

As you know, the world's largest store has some of the world's bigest events. But this week at Macy*s, there's a small and special show you should see.

If you're expecting Uncle Joe or Cousin Sally this summer, now's the time to investigate the remarkable collection of sofa-beds at Macy*s. What makes them really remarkable is that you'd never guess they're sofa beds at all.

Do you consider cooking an art? Then Macy*s Carrier Cook Shop will fascinate you. For here you can buy the professional tools that make the difference between cooking and cuisine.

Macy*s recently fed some data into a computer and came up with an interesting fact. Every seven and one quarter minutes of every day, Macy*s installs another broadloom in another home.

Here's a riddle for you. What Mother's Day gift is so unusual that you probably haven't thought of it . . yet it's a gift Mother would welcome... a gift Macy*s has in profusion? The answer? A chair all her own.

Is it really worth the difference to have your draperies custom-made?

Sometimes art can improve on nature. Take the daisies that are in full bloom at Macy*s now. Not one of them is real, but every one's a beauty.

This started as a gimmick. Macy*s said they had so many kinds of pillows they could go straight down the alphabet describing them... and still not describe all. So they began. Abstract art pillows, brocaded pillows. . . . . .

If you think one oval braided rug looks like another oval braided rug, you obviously haven't been to Macy*s lately.

Note 1. Despite the indirect and longish lead-ins (OK because these were 1-minute commercials), there was a specific piece of merchandise and its price in every one.

Note 2. This was a campaign. With a change of language (to relate to the merchandise), every commercial ended "For this is one of the pleasures of shopping at Macy*s. The abundance you find, whether it's braided rugs or practically anything else." Except for this sign-off, there were NO generalities. If generalities are a waste of space in the newspapers, they are even more ineffective on the air.

The Sale Commercial

A sale commercial should have urgency, believability, and sell the savings. Just like a sale ad. Like a sale ad, the more you can limit the time of the event, the more powerful. Here is the way you might do a 30-second mink coat sale. Notice how little description there is of the merchandise. The push is to bring customers in tomorrow.

Tomorrow... and tomorrow only... at Jones's... buy a natural mink coat at a fraction of today's price. Yes, tomorrow... full length natural mink coats for $1100. They'll go right back up to their regular $1500 price Thursday. So come to Jone's tomorrow.. See these marvelous mink coats. Choose the color you want, the style you love... and save. Remember Jones's one-day sale-price... just $1100 for full length natural mink coats. Tomorrow only. Come early for the most beautiful buys!

A storewide sale? Just as direct. (These assume no "handle" to the sale.)

10-second ID:

It starts tomorrow! Jones's spring sale. See aisles of bargains. Hundreds of buys. Sale after sale after sale... tremendous savings wherever you turn. Jones's Spring sale... starting tomorrow. Don't miss it!

30-second:

It starts tomorrow! Jones's Spring Sale. See aisles of bargains... hundreds of buys. Sale after sale after sale... tremendous savings wherever you turn. A manufacturer's closeout of children's shoes. A clearance of men's sweaters at half price. Handbags that are regularly $21... tomorrow only 15.99 at Jones's. And these are just a few of the many, many exciting sales waiting for you. Come save tomorrow. . . . In Jones's Spring Sale. Open til nine p.m.

Note 1. Even though the sale may go on and on, don't mention it. Bring them in tomorrow. If you say "two week sale", you'll never get them.

Note 2. A sale commercial, like a sale ad, is more effective with specific merchandise in it, except possibly in an ID where you could only mention one item which limits the feeling of scope. One or two prices are about as much as the listener can understand, so use other ways of conveying value as well.

Suggested Copy

If you buy time on a radio show where the personality does the commercial, you may be asked for a spec sheet rather than a script. Just make sure that you indicate emphasis...or you may find that the zippered section on the handbag gets a big play and the creamy dreamy leather is not mentioned at all.

The Taped Commercial

It costs more, but it gives you many advantages.

You can rehearse a commercial, so every inflection is just right and the emphasis is precisely where you want it.

You can use sound effects and music. In fact, you can do your whole commercial in song, if you wish.

But the *greatest advantage of the taped commercial is that you can use two voices.* Properly handled, two voices are more than twice as attention-getting as a single voice. Why? Probably because the listener feels like an eavesdropper. . and that's irresistible.

Proper handling means that the voices and the message *must* be conversational. A single announcer can get away with a phrase like "a remarkable opportunity to save", but you can't put that into anybody's mouth when you have two voices. The voices must represent people, and speak like people.

The one-minute spot is usually better than 30 seconds for two voices because it lets you develop two personalities, which adds to the memorability of your commercials. (Holding the listener's interest through a solid 60 seconds with one voice is far from easy.) Also, you must be conversational, and it takes more words to be conversational.

Instead of starting with "What better gift for your Father than a new golf ball", you break the idea into conversation:

she: What are we giving Dad for Father's Day?

he: How about a golf jacket?

she: That's what we gave him last year.

he: Oh? Well, there are some new golf balls I've meant to try.

Always try to have a little drama or contrast in your personalities. (Think of them as real people when you write.) Play the timid against the try-anything, the Doubting Thomas against the know-it-all, the woman against her mother-in-law, the young against the old, etc. Incidentally, radio is the place for humor, if that's your beat. To be funny in print doesn't work well. But on radio!

Trick: If you have a limited budget, and there's no union problem, you don't need professional actors. Use the two best voices in your store. Some really great commercials have been taped by amateurs.

If, for example, you have merchants with good voices, use them. Let them tell the public who they are and why they bought the merchandise.

Very convincing.

Jingles, music, sound effects

Let's dispose of jingles, first of all. Great for Pan Am, ineffective for a store. Why? A jingle obscures the message. Pan Am can afford to be on the air day after day, hour after hour. So after a while the listener can understand every word. Rare when you have only a handful of commercials.

Music, however, is an excellent way to gain identification. Especially music that's used consistently so it becomes a theme song. This music can have words (always the same words, if possible) as long as you don't rely on those words to do your selling.

Example: Your Christmas ads have all been thought out. Now you've been asked to translate them for radio. You decide that a few bars of music at the beginning are needed to get attention. You either choose some music that's in the public domain (otherwise you'll be paying fat royalties) or that your radio station owns. You can use just the music, or add some general words to them: "Jones, your Christmas store on every floor". A sort of repeated musical slogan.

Sound effects can also be stoppers and identification for the store. Anything from a bird call to cymbals clashing.

CHAPTER 19

TV: "THE MEDIUM IS NOT THE MESSAGE"

This is a quote from Duke Marx, who's the president of the Marx Advertising Agency and Film Co. in Milwaukee. He says he spends a good part of his time persuading clients that they're not in show biz. A commercial is not meant to entertain, but to sell. Don't worry about making a playlet or a comedy out of your commercial, but concentrate on selling.

A television commercial is not a radio commercial with pictures. TV provides action. It involves the viewer in a demonstration of merchandise... rather than a description in words.

In its way, a TV commercial is a 3-ring circus. You have (1) *the video:* the picture. (2) *the audio:* the sound. (3) *the super:* the words superimposed on the picture.

Before we discuss writing for TV, you ought to know a few things.

Most retail commercials do not have the actors speaking. Instead they use "voice over", an announcer talking while the picture is showing. This is a matter of dollars, of production time, and of flexibility. (If Jones's has stores in Boston, Hartford, and New Haven, they can super the names Jones's and the voice can name a different branch store in each market.)

The least expensive TV spots are slides, one after the next, with supers on some, and voice over.

Why do we keep mentioning expense? Because a 30-second TV commercial costs from $3,000 to $5,000. For production alone. This doesn't even include air time.

Which is why so many stores turn to outside advertising agencies or TV production companies to create their commercials. Or they buy canned commercials, sometimes for as little as $50 a throw. However, the stores' copywriters are getting more involved in writing the scripts. For even if you've never written one before, as a copywriter, you know much more about your store, its merchandise, and its point of view than an outsider.

On the other hand, you cannot merely write an audio and let somebody else take over. In no other medium is there such a marriage of word and picture. You must either do both audio and video yourself, or you must work directly with the person doing the video and the producer of the commercial. You can, however, fit words to an existing video without trouble.

What should you keep in mind when you're writing a TV commercial?

1. *You must have a balance between audio, video, and supers.* If you make them all work too hard, you'll distract rather than sell. Try to look at a pretty pair of legs climbing stairs in panty hose, reading a super that says 3 pairs for 2.90 today only, and listen to an announcer enumerating 6 colors. You absorb nothing.

2. *Let the video carry as much of the story as it can,* using words only to underline, give emphasis, customer benefits, information the picture can't provide. If you were writing a print ad about a winter coat, you'd say "warm" somewhere. Your TV picture shows a man whistling through a blizzard. You don't need the word "warm".

3. *Be as brief as you can.* If this means writing disconnected phrases rather than complete sentences, fine. Most people don't talk in sentences, anyway. Don't say "Today is a great day for you to buy your washer". Say "Today...a great day...to buy your washer."

4. *Like white space on an ad, there should be breathing space on TV*...time when there's no audio and the viewer can concentrate on the picture.

5. *When you're writing an audio to accompany slides,* don't write so much copy for any slide that it just sits there and sits

and sits. Audio and video must both maintain a lively, interesting pace.

6. *You don't need a ballet or a soap opera to* catch your audience. Never forget...what a retail store has to say is news. (And if *you've* forgotten, see Chapter 2. What was said about newspapers is, fortunately, true of all media.) Get right into your message, show what you're selling, tell them about it...and get off the tube. This is what Duke Marx means by the medium is not the message.

7. *Ask your TV station who your audience is. .* and write to it.

8. *As in radio, you must consider the sound of words* rather than the way they look on your typewritten page. It's even more important on TV, because your audience is looking at a picture and listening at the same time.

9. *Within these limitations, every principle of writing good copy applies.*

Now let's take a few examples.

We saw how the golf ball ad became a radio spot. Here's the 30-second TV commercial:

AUDIO	VIDEO
This is Macy*s XP 270. The new golf ball that adds 4 yards to 12 yards to your drive. Every time.	Hand putting ball on tee (show ball marking XP/270) Ball hit by driver (close-up)
Tested by Macy*s Bureau of Standards it traveled further.	repeat
Further than the best-known top-quality balls.	repeat
In the laboratory. On the golf course. Time after time.	repeat
Ball after ball.	repeat

4 yards to 12 yards
further.
Test it yourself.
Macy*s XP/270
developed by MacGregor.
Amazing.

Show cover of box of
balls and ball

Super: Macy*s XP/270
    box of twelve, $10
Super: Phone Macy*s(big)

Notice how the commercial gives the news, the customer benefit, the urge to action, the up-beat ending. The name of the ball is in the audio and on a super, so it can be seen as well as heard. Ditto Macy*s. There's only about 20 seconds worth of copy, so there's 10 seconds breathing space to distribute.

To show you how little copy you really need on familiar merchandise, here are 3 audios from a 20-second TV series. The idea was to expose a lot of goods, and sell the idea of Macy*s as a place to buy gifts. The video, in each, was a Macy logo at start and finish, a film showing the merchandise, and the vendor's logo and price superimposed where appropriate.

Another great gift idea from Macy*s
Stretchini tights...
UP-tights... of Monsanto Actionwear nylon...
Nine colors...
Three pairs... for six seventy-five
Macy*s has <u>great</u> ideas for Christmas

Another great gift idea from Macy*s...
Something special...
A four-piece silverplate coffee set...
by Oneida.
Serves six.
Specially priced... just twenty-four
ninety-nine.
Macy*s has <u>great</u> ideas for Christmas

Another great gift idea from Macy*s...
Starflight molded luggage...

only at Macy*s
Colorful...rugged...
washable inside and out...
For just fifty dollars...take two
to go...Anywhere!
Macy*s has <u>great</u> gift ideas for Christmas

The Ready-Made Commercial

Commercials can be rented or bought from some of the larger manufacturers and from companies whose business it is to produce such commercials. What you usually get is a film with a music track on it, a suggested script to be read by your local announcer, and a story board so you can develop your own script. Often you also get a manufacturer's logo to superimpose and you can also super your own logo, prices, etc.

Most stores can't even begin to afford the professional quality film they can get this way.

To make the commercial your own, a new script must be written. Tacking your store's name at the end is not as effective a selling tool.

Here are 2 visually superb commercials produced HF/TV in High Point, N.C. a few years ago. I will describe the video, give their script, then a script as you might write it. (Their scripts are not bad—merely general... of necessity.)

1-minute warehouse sale. Video shows a quartet of pretty models in pants suits, driving to store, then acting like warehouse personnel getting merchandise ready for the big sale. This is the suggested script:

The smartest women in town know...the smartest
time to dress up their home is now...because
(your store's) bigger-than-ever Warehouse Sale
is on. (Your store) needs room for new stock, so
you can save on furniture from America's finest
manufacturers. (Your store) offers big savings

in every department for every room in your home... up to 30 percent. Magnificent dining rooms, bedrooms in every style. Don't miss (your store's) outstanding Warehouse Sale. Join the smartest women in town!

Here is a retail translation. Video remains the same.

Where is everybody going? To Jones's. Why? Because Jones's Warehouse Sale starts today. With bigger-than-ever bargains for your home. Joneses is sweeping its warehouse clean... to make room for new stock. That's why you save so much on furniture by some of the country's top makers. Magnificent dining rooms, bedroom sets by the dozens... even one five-piece set for a surprising 30% off. And so much more. Don't miss Jones's tremendous warehouse sale. Come join the crowd... and save plenty!

The difference? Fewer generalities. A more staccato tempo. Greater urgency.

30-seconds on Timely Clothes for men:

Video	Suggested Script	New Script
Beef-eater in full regalia	Some clothes are classics	Some men's clothes are classics
3 men and a girl walking abreast	Some clothes are timely! Store Name invites you to join the Changeables	Some are timely. Like the new fashion collection you'll see at Jones's
Same group getting into a sports car	Store Name knows the Changeables won't settle for a single look, a single style in men's fashions	Because Jones's knows there's no one look, no one style today... but many..

Close-up of man alongside car	They demand body-line shapes, modern translations, western styling	From the new body-hugging double-breasteds to updated westerns
3 men and girl on bikes. Timely supered	They find them at Store Name in contemporary suits, jackets and slacks by Timely Clothes	All at Jones's now in contemporary suits, jackets and slacks by Timely Clothes
group interestingly posed, store name supered	Join the Changeables. Develop a new personal identity with Timely Clothes, now at Store Name.	Come see them and try them today.. the new Timely Clothes at Jones's. For your life style.

What we have done here is simple...but what a difference it makes. We've taken the abstraction "The Changeables" and turned it into "you". And added the good old retail prod: come see, come try.

CHAPTER 20

PLEASE SEND ME

Selling by mail, whether it's a 200-page catalogue or a card telling a handful of customers that a new shipment of Brie has arrived, is called direct mail (or direct marketing).

However, there's direct mail and more direct mail.

Retail direct mail differs from that of a catalogue house or a solicitation for the latest magazine on ecology. Our customers can usually come in and see the merchandise if they choose.

Like all retail advertising, there's a need to sell the store as well as the merchandise. *You're not buying from the mailing piece, you're buying from the store.*

Direct mail has grown to include things that never even see a post office. Like inserts and sections. Prepared by the store (insert) or the paper (section) and distributed by the newspaper.

There's also direct mail that is basically an invitation to come see the goods. Rather than asking the customer to order it then and there. Here we'll be dealing primarily with direct mail that's also direct response.

        Catalogues, Booklets, Inserts, Sections

Selling by mail and/or phone has a built-in advantage. You don't compete for the customer's attention. No other store's ads on the next page. No world news. Does this mean you can merely list the facts, like a specification sheet? Hardly. You still have to do a strong selling job, you still must persuade the customer to buy.

Good direct mail copy has the sell of any other advertising: the customer benefits, the reasons to buy at your store, the "you" approach, the news, the translation of technical details into lay language, the urgency. Naturally there are special problems... and special solutions.

1. *You must make it easy for the customer to order.* That means all the facts. Saying "green and 5 other fashion colors:" won't get you any business from a customer who prefers blue or yellow. Dimensions, fabric content, sizes, washability (if it's a factor), trimming, even how-to-use and whether or not it comes knocked-down, if they apply.

2. *Your coupon must be big enough* for the customer to use comfortably. And ordering instructions must be clear, not filled with gobbledegook. Read it and ask yourself if the dumbest bunny you know could follow them.

3. *Space is limited, so you must be brief.* There is rarely room for padding, for qualifying adjectives, for creating a mood within the captions.

From the Ward's book I'll discuss later:

"Short jumpsuit in beige and white acetate lace bonded to acetate tricot. Tie sash, button front. Machine wash, tumble dry."

"2-pc. cotton and stretch nylon terry bikini. Lightly padded bra with adjustable straps, back hooked. Bikini pants lined in front. Elastic waist, legs. Multi-stripe."

No "beautifuls", no "wear it anywhere". Just facts.

4. *If your copy is not directly under each item,* you must use some form of keying that makes identification unmistakable. A key letter on the art and starting your copy is much clearer than "reading from right to left" or "clockwise".

5. *If it's fashion merchandise and it's not on models,* quickly tell the reader whom it's for. Boys' cotton shorts. Junior skirt.

Children's boot. Don't ask them to wade through the copy till they get to sizes.

With these restrictions, how is it possible to sell effectively? By the generous use of ideas...on the cover, in headlines, and editorials.

Cover

Your booklet cover should not be a label, unless perhaps you have an illustration so provocative, so illuminating that it's self-explanatory. The exception is Christmas. If you have a Christmas illustration and say "Christmas at Jones's", you don't need much more. The reader knows this is the booklet that has gift ideas.

Your cover should say something. Make the reader want to sit right down and read your booklet. What should it say? Consider a booklet cover as the headline for an ad, and let it give the reason for buying, or the customer benefit. Then develop it.

Don't just say "Summer at Jones's". Or even "Summer Sale". Instead:

```
Summer begins right here
         with a welcome collection of ideas
         to make your summer more fun
```

beach people. backyard people. mountain people. golf people. barbecue people. weekend people. boat people. hammock people.
          JONES'S SUMMER SALE IS
            FOR SUMMER PEOPLE

Come preview
Jones's summer sale
12 pages of summer fashions.... sale-priced

10 pages of summer furniture.... sale-priced
6 pages of good summer ideas.... sale-priced
Shop them before we tell the public about these big summer buys

If your booklet is not a sale booklet, and many are not, then your cover should be as editorial as possible. Like a magazine cover. Let's go back to "Summer begins right here" and see what we might add to the cover:

>   *Learn a dozen new ways to keep your cool*
>   *Beach preview: more cover-up is more alluring*
>   *Invite a crowd and have an easy cookout*
>   *The flowery fragrances of summer*

Headlines

What a booklet is *not* is a series of individual ads. Your page headlines should have a family relationship and, of course, stem from the merchandise. Since booklets are often conglomerates, with everything from lingerie to toasters, this is a bit of a trick. (You can often get off the horns of your dilemma by relying on the graphics to provide the family relationship.) It can result in headlines so general they're a waste of space. a) "Spring Cleaning Aids". b) "Fashions for your season in the sun". c) "Little notions can mean a lot".

Let's turn these 3 clunks into page headlines that work.

a) "Before you start Spring cleaning, check these." (the you approach)

b) "Pink satin shorts? Why not?" (or whatever your fashion story is)

c) "Use the coupon or phone today. . it's the easiest way to get ready for summer". This ignores the merchandise. When you can't get a good selling headline out of the goods, tell a store story: hours, credit, write or phone, preview idea, idea, assortment. It's a better use of space than a generality.

Editorials

Since you don't need giant-sized type in a booklet to attract attention, you find you often have space for a short editorial in addition to, or instead of, a headline. Or you lead off with a few lines before your captions. This is your opportunity to sell your store, your merchandise, your ideas. One or all. It resembles the general copy of an ad, only briefer. It spells out customer benefits and your superiorities.

Let's make it difficult. Let's assume you have a page of girl's accessories in a back-to-school booklet: 2 handbags, 1 scarf, 1 pr. mittens, 1 pr. gloves, 1 knit hat, 2 pcs. costume jewelry, 1 petticoat. Here are 2 ways to handle the editorial.

a) the reason for buying at your store:

Mothers and daughters agree: shopping to go back to school is more fun at Jones's. More exciting fashions, more sensible prices. That's how we bridge the generation gap.

b) the merchandise and assortment story:

We're ready for school now. With all the essentials. And the frivolities. From the newest shoulder bags to the maddest mittens. Start here, then come see all the other goodies waiting for your daughter at Jones's.

A page of related merchandise is easier. Your editorial is a mini-ad.

The Sale Booklet

Don't rely on the SALE on your cover. The sale and saving idea must be continued on every page, in your headlines, your editorials, captions.

Do you have a window? Here are easy-care Dacron ninon curtains to fit it. . sale-priced now

Our lowest price in 3 years for cotton percale sheets with posies

Pick a pair of pillows. . extra large, superbly comfortable, non-allergenic. . and 28% less than regular prices

Big special purchase of ready-to-assemble furniture

Save $60 on full-size sofa-beds in costly crushed velvet

Note: Some of these are longer than newspaper ad headlines would be. However, any one would make a good newspaper sale ad. Which is the answer to the sale booklet. Follow the rules for creating a good sale ad, and you'll have a strong sale booklet.

The New Breed of Direct Mail

In the Spring of 1970, Montgomery Ward produced a 75-page catalogue that shattered tradition. The cover showed a young couple in a very un-posed pose. All it said was "The Unexpected Generation".

Inside, it was full of surprises, in graphics and copy. There wasn't one straight staid catalogue shot, but groups of young people in action or unusual still lifes. Not one picture-caption, picture-caption page. And many pages had fairly long editorials.

A page of beach clothes was headed "SCUBA ARUBA". Then. . .

"Water is its own environment. It changes people. Ever notice the timid secretary when she hits the beach? Or the mild-mannered junior executive when he starts talking about his scuba gear? Water is natural. Unstructured. Observe it. Or get into it. It can be your other environment. Or your primary one". .

Captions were straight catalogue copy.

The book was superbly merchandised. While primarily a fashion booklet for young people, all the atmosphere merchandise, from flippers to rugs, was captioned and priced. Even the antique-style phone on the how-to-order page had a description and price.

The catalogue was extraordinarily successful. So suddenly the off-beat catalogue became the in thing to do. Like the Famous-Barr Anniversary Sale in the form of a paper-back book. After all, there's no reason why a catalogue must be a catalogue the way it's always been.

Computers are also changing direct mail. First by breaking down mailing lists into small, very special audiences. Properly programmed, your computer can print out a list of people with 3 cars or women who dye their hair or families with incomes over $25,000. Anything.

This makes direct mail more economical, since you send your piece only to those who are potentially interested in it. As a copywriter, it makes your job easier. You know your audience.

Then there's the computer letter, a bit of electronic wizardry whereby the name of the person you're addressing can be used within the letter. No "dear neighbor" or "dear customer", but "dear Mrs. Smith". And you can even say things like. . "No wonder, Mrs. Smith, we think. . ." It's fascinating, because it takes any letter out of the form letter category. You really talk to Mrs. Smith, person-to-person.

The Shopper

The growth of shopping centers has resulted in the burgeoning of center "newspapers" and mailing pieces. They consist of ads from the stores in the shopping center. They differ from newspapers only because there's no news. Your ad should be a good newspaper ad, with strong store identification. If the customers come to you first, they may never get to the competition.

The Private Sale

This is an event for a selected list of the store's charge customers. It may be a letter or a folder or a series of inserts. (Some stores have been sending out an envelope full of individual sheets, each with its own sale.) Strangely enough, a gimmick often gives this kind of mailing added strength. What kind of a gimmick? A discount card, usable only that day or night. A telegram format. A tag for the customer. An unexpected idea.

What's important in your copy?

1. The private idea.... your privilege to shop this private sale. A highly productive private sale was once based on "Classified Information".

2. Clear and quick identification of where, what, and when.

3. The implication that, at this sale, the prices are lower than usual. If this is true, point out that prices will go back up again after the sale.

Plus, of course, good sound sale copy. Since this is an event customers must come to, keep it brief. Just enough facts to bring them in.

CHAPTER 21
MARKETING

This is the new game in town. Even though marketing is probably as old as commerce. When a caveman had three extra bearskins or an ancient Egyptian a spare bushel of millet and they went looking for takers, this was a primitive form of marketing. Matching the right product to the right customer at the right time.

It's only in this century that marketing has become an organized discipline. (Although marketing experts are still arguing whether it's an art or a science.) Statistical analysis is being substituted for seat of the pants decisions.

Until recently, marketing was a way of doing business only for the giants with gigantic distribution: the soap makers, the car manufacturers, and their ilk. Retailers resisted the marketing approach. Their reasoning was that, by the time the market research was done and analyzed, their market place would have changed. They thought in terms of "Should we buy pink or blue this Spring", instead of "How can we reach the married working woman". They felt they were too volatile, too small, and that they really knew their market better than any outsider.

All this has changed recently. If you look at the tables of organization of large department stores, you'll find that chief of the advertising department in many of them is now a marketing person. Rather than a sales promotion director. Granted some of these changes are purely cosmetic; marketing director is a jazzier title these days than sales promotion director. In others, however, it's a real change of attitude and approach. And their numbers are increasing.

So much for history. What, then is marketing? In the broadest (and simplest) terms, it's selling more things to more people. Anticipating demand, increasing demand, satisfying demand. Sometimes even creating demand. Not only can products be marketed, but also services... and even political candidates.

Advertising is only one function of marketing. It's a total package that includes everything from pricing to operating strategy.

In a store, the marketing director usually works with both merchants and advertising. Defining the market for merchants so they know for whom they're buying. Rather than instinctively buying because "they'll like it". Telling the advertising people whom they're talking to. The whole demographic bit. And through which media they can best be reached. Helping the store plan for the future.

With market research, a store can find out who it is (you'd be surprised how many of them don't know). and who its customer are, who its non-customers are and why, and what customers think of them. It can position itself vis-à-vis competition, find its special niche and exploit it.

All of which information comes in mighty handy when you sit down to turn out a bit of good selling prose. You know whom you're talking to.

You don't have to become a marketing expert yourself, but it would pay you to get hold of a college text on marketing and read it. Don't be put off by the language: randomized, input-output analysis, psychographic profiles and like jargon. Part of it comes out of statistics, part of it they've had to invent as they went along to accommodate new concepts. There are some fascinating ideas buried under what I, at least, consider poor writing.

Marketing for retailers is here to stay. You might as well become familiar with it right now.

CHAPTER 22
A COPYWRITER'S LOT

One day, for my own amusement, (and the amazement of the class I teach at the Tobe-Coburn School) I listed the things a copywriter is called upon to write....other than copy and commercials:
Signs, posters, brochures, booklets, invitations, billboards, mailing pieces, letters, speeches (for VIPs), employee bulletins, presentations, sales-training material, merchandise tags, post-mortems, information sheets, fashion show commentaries, contest blanks, Christmas cards...and even skits for store parties. In some stores, copywriters do publicity releases as well.

Why all these? Because every message that reaches a customer should pass through a copywriter's typewriter. To make sure that it becomes a selling message. The shoe buyer may be an expert, but when he tries to write a letter about a private sale, he usually ends up with an awkward, involved, badly written piece. Also, as was noted in Chapter 12, to a great extent, the copywriter is the store's image. And, presumably, the copywriter is a professional...one who can write any kind of prose. Well.

Most of the writing jobs listed are sometime things. Signs, posters, and letters are everyday.

Posters

1. *Be brief.* Your story is read at a glance...a passing glance at that.
2. *Be staccato.* Don't write complete sentences.
3. *Dramatize* the one most important fact.
4. *Stay in character.* . with the event and your store.

5. *Don't be cute.* You'll hate yourself after you've seen the sign for the 32nd time. Cuteness doesn't wear well.

Wrong:	*Right:*
Santa Claus is now in our new Snowland on the 2nd floor. Bring your children to meet him today.	Santa Claus? Of course! Snowland, 2nd floor

Wrong:	*Right:*
Whether you need a dozen sheets or a pair of napkins, now's the time to buy them in Jones's White Sale	Save now! Jones's White Sale

If your poster has more than 5 or 6 words (plus a location line) ....try again. There are exceptions, to be sure, but most posters can be brief. Think of them as a well-designed headline.

Window Signs

These are short news messages. They are not posters, they are not ads, but an editorial comment on the window's contents. They have one purpose. To make the passerby come into the store. The customer can't buy from the window, so you don't need details. Nor do you need any store build-up. If the merchandise and your message interest them, they'll come in even if they hate you.

THE NEW PIONEERS
Mary Smith ruffles up the prettiest calicoes this side of the late-show Westerns. See them in Vogue, see them on Jones's 2nd floor. Junior sizes 7 to 11.

MEET ESTORADO BY DREXEL
Inspired by the handsome country-homes of Portugal, built with the care you expect from

Drexel. See 3 interesting room settings starring Estorado on Jones's 2nd floor.

If you have Names, use them. If you have third party endorsement by a magazine or a newspaper, use it. And always give a floor or department. As a customer as well as a copywriter, you usually would like to see prices in the window. If your display department considers individual price signs inartistic, have another smaller sign listing all of them.

Letters

1. *Be warm and friendly.* Forget that you are a store and write person to person.

2. *Don't include long lists of merchandise and or prices.* A few are OK. They don't belong in a letter. Put them on an enclosure, on the back of the letter, or make your letter a double fold with the letter on the outside, and your inventory inside.

3. *Keep in mind the person who's signing the letter.* If it's the store president or manager, stay away from little details. He's not likely to describe colors and sizes and prices. Be big.

4. *The lead sentence is the most difficult one to write.* Stay away from the tired beginnings: "It is my pleasure to"... "I thought you'd like to know". Stay away from the oblique approach. "As I was walking down the street today". Instead, make believe you're writing to your favorite uncle. Or else get right into the story.

5. *Personalize.* Sprinkle your letter with "I" and "we".

Getting Information

In the table of organization of a store, the ad department is a service department. A tool for buyers, merchants, stylists. But there's a mutual interdependence. An ad is only as good as the information the copywriter gets.

A copywriter writes many departments...the smaller the store, the more departments...and can't be an expert in every category of merchandise. An information sheet that only says "black polyester crepe, sizes 10-18, 59.99", doesn't help. Even if the copywriter has seen the dress. It may be that the buyer believes clinging crepes are going to be hot items and this ad is her feeler. Only the buyers know precisely why they bought the merchandise. Without this information, the copywriter is left in limbo.

Copywriters generally get their information 1) at meetings when merchandise for a week's or month's advertising is shown and discussed 2) from meetings with individual buyers 3) from printed advertising request forms buyers fill out. Method (2) is by far the best, but if you're stuck with (1) or (3), use the phone. Talk to buyers whenever you can (not assistants because that stretches the line of communication). After you've seen the goods, so you can talk intelligently.

Problem Buyers

Every store has a few. Chronically late with information sheets and/or proofs. Or prone to exaggeration (every sale is our biggest ever) and useless generalities. Or too busy (or too indifferent) to return your calls. Or the ad expert; he writes an ad on the information sheet instead of giving you facts. Then is piqued if you don't use it verbatim. (He probably got A- in English Composition and considers himself a Writer.)

How do you cope with them? Actually the problem sorts itself out into two parts. The kind management should help with. And the kind you must handle solo. If buyers are always late or unavailable, even uncooperative, keep a record of this. Then tell your superior. Advertising is part of a buyer's job. It's up to management to see that it's done.

The others? What's called for is a combination of ego massage and education. By you. They simply don't understand what good copy is and how important they are to ads you write. There's nobody to teach them unless you (and other ad people do.)*

Buyers' lack of understanding so often causes poor advertising that M.L. Rosenblum and I have written a book for them. "The Secret Ingredient of Good Retail Ads: A Handbook for Buyers and Their Bosses" (NRMA)

Getting Okays

Your copy comes back from the buyer with two words crossed out of the headline, all the colors and prices changed, the maker of the thread that goes into the yarn that becomes the fabric is added, and one sentence rewritten in bad English.

Do you get angry or stubbornly refuse to change a word? No. First you change colors and prices. These are facts, and facts must be correct...even if you were given the wrong ones to start off with. You add the thread-maker. He's probably paying for half the ad. Then you call the buyer and ask why the other changes.

If your point of view is wrong ... the important thing about these panties is that they come up to size XXL and you buried this information...or forgot that it's the built-in bread board that makes the bread-box unique...you rewrite your headline and as much of the ad as necessary.

If the problem is language...well, then you've got a problem. Everybody thinks he's a writer. You must gently persuade the buyer that writing is your job. He wouldn't tell a surgeon how to do an appendectomy, would he? (Once in a while, the complaint is legitimate. You're talking above the heads of customers or down to them or not using the word that's the real key word. Make the change.)

Trick: Ask "What should we say instead?" Chances are the buyer will flounder around, offer a few suggestions at which you raise your eyebrows. Then you suggest a word or phrase. Not your original one, not any of his. A completely new one. It's almost always accepted with relief.

Correcting Proofs

It's difficult to proof-read your own copy. You know what it says. You often can't see the typographical errors. So read for sense, then read word for word. You may find you have to fill a line or cut a line. Try to do this as close to the bottom of the ad as possible. Your newspaper may charge for extensive changes.

Moreover, if you only get one proof and you have a whole paragraph reset, you'll never see it . . and it may appear in the paper with errors. Try to cut words rather than rewrite, if you can. Filling a line is no problem. It's a skill you acquire. And you'll acquire it!

There's a standard set of symbols for correcting proofs that's used by writers, production people, proofreaders, and typographers. It's a sort of shorthand everybody understands. Use it and your intentions are perfectly clear. Incidentally, if you make changes on your typed manuscript, use these symbols, too... and avoid confusion.

Here are the most commonly used of these proofreaders' marks and what they mean. Your production department or newspaper can give you a whole list of others.

ℓ take out	# space between lines
∧ insert at this point	-/ hyphen
⊙ period	¶ make paragraph
,/ comma	no ¶ no paragraph
:/ colon	stet let it stand
;/ semi-colon	tr transpose
∨/ apostrophe	caps caps
⌠ space between words	ℓ.c. lower-case letter

Besides using proofreaders' marks when you correct manuscript or proofs, there are two other conventions. Always draw your corrections out to the margin, and circle them so they can be seen and read. Needless to say, they should be written in your most careful script. This is how you do it.

Sale ~~12.99~~ to 29.99   (14.99)
Summer lingerie at
— remarkable savings
A glorious collection, from tailored to
frothy. At glorious low prices. Come
gather ~~panties,~~ nightdresses, pajamas,
~~robes~~. Nylons, polyesters, even some   (robes)
cottons. We bought out a manufacturers
whole stock to bring you this buy. So
come on the run. Sizes 10 to 18.

CHAPTER 23

STORE NAME GOES HERE

It's called co-operative advertising. It's called vendor-paid advertising. It's called partially-paid for advertising. It's called a boon... and murder.

What is it?

It's advertising that's paid for by the manufacturer or distributor in one of several forms.

1. The manufacturer provides mats or glossy proofs (actually complete ads, ready to go to the papers). Your store may pay for the newspaper space or not, depending on arrangements made by your merchants.

2. The manufacturer gives an advertising allowance against sales. The more you sell, the larger the dollar amount, since it's usually a percentage. You use the money to advertise his products.

3. The manufacturer pays (all or partially) on proof of performance: a tear sheet of the ad.

And so on. This is a merchant-vendor arrangement, so how it happens doesn't concern you. But how it appears in the newspaper does.

It's human to resent a mat, or manufacturer's suggestions on copy and art and layout, and requirements that his name be in the largest type in the ad, his logo to be a certain size, or whatever. You think you know how to make a better ad. You may. But consider this. If the vendor didn't pay for the advertising, chances are that the ads wouldn't be in the paper. If vendors didn't pay for pages in booklets, you might have skinny little folders instead of fat catalogues. From the store's point of view, these are plus advertising dollars, extra exposure.

The question is: how do you make co-op copy your own? If a store is paying you as a copywriter, it's a waste of your salary and talents to toss a manufacturer's ad into the newspaper and just add the store's name. No matter how busy you are.

A manufacturer's ad is prepared for hundreds of stores. It's written in the most general terms. It cannot have your store personality. It's almost always set in a different type face.

If the art is better than your store can afford to buy, or you have no staff artist, then use the art part of the mat or reproduction proof. (If you're lucky, you may even get a separate proof that's just art.) Then rewrite the ad in your language, your style; use your type face, talk to your customers. Your version should out-pull the original sufficiently to pay for your day's work. And become part of the impression the reader has of your store.

I can prove this. By now, Sardo is so successful that it's a staple, and I'm sure the Sardo people won't mind my telling this story.

When I was copy chief at Gimbels New York, our store was chosen to launch Sardo, the first bath oil. A whole Sardo committee came in with an ad they wanted us to use. The headline was "Revolutionary New Discovery". The type was wall-to-wall with a mass of semi-scientific jargon. With, of course, a spot at the bottom for Gimbels name.

I was tempted to tell them to go peddle their wares some place else, but the product seemed so good (and the ad allowance so tempting), that I tried persuasion. We finally compromised. Their ad would run in the Sunday News, with the Gimbel logo. We would run our own ad in the now defunct Sunday Tribune, which had a circulation of about $1/6$ that of the News.

Both ads had coupons. Our ad was a drawing of a pretty girl in a Victorian bath tub, and a small picture of the bottle. Our headline was "No body but no body is smoother than the body that comes out of a Sardo bath", with lighthearted benefit copy. It pulled over 1,000 coupons and sold every other bottle we had in stock over the counter. Their ad? Not a single coupon. A bomb.

Some vendors merely ask that you do a good ad, and use their name. Good for them. They usually get the most for their money.

Others will hem you in with all kinds of specifications on type sizes and logotypes and even language.

These restrictions should be no more confining or irritating than any other restrictions you work with. Handle the ad like a regular ad, noting the vendor's requirements along with your facts.

It's up to the merchants to give you this information since they made the deal with the vendor. (If you're smart, you'll question some of this, especially the use of manufacturer logotypes. You may find the buyer is just trying to be nice to a nice vendor and has made no committments.)

Then there's the vendor who comes in personally, sits on your desk, and gives you a sales talk. Fine...until he pulls out a piece of copy he just happened to write on his way downtown. Take it, ease him off your desk, and write your own ad.

Trick: The vendor may require that his name be set in type as large as your headline type. If it's a great name, no problem. You'd want to use it. But what if it's Mr. Great Unknown? Write the headline that tells your story. Then your copy. Then *another* headline (to be set in the same size type as your heading) to go under the copy, including his name. A sandwich. For example, you might have a collection of new tee shirts from TNT. The shirts are unusual and exciting but TNT is a cipher to your readers. Your headline could be "You've never seen tees like these". Then body copy. Then, in the same size type as your headline, "All by TNT... dynamite!" Which keeps you from cluttering your own heading or writing a label.

Manufacturer's Aids

The larger manufacturers will be glad to fill your arms with booklets, pamphlets, folders, glossy photographs, specification sheets, etc. They're helpful, but...be warned. Most of these are not pitched for the consumer...or even for you. They are meant for the trade, for buyers. Do not pick up the language. Translate it for the customer.

If you don't know what a wedge frame is on a bike, don't just copy it from a spec sheet. Your reader won't know either. Have the buyer explain it and describe it in your language.

Be warned again. Most of this literature (even when consumer-oriented) will be filled with dangerous superlatives. Naturally, he thinks his product is the best. That's all he sells. But you may sell 16 other brands of the same thing. If you say the XYZ stereo is the best stereo made...what does that say about your stock of 15 other stereo brands?

CHAPTER 24

MONEY, MONEY, MONEY!

Until you get to be a copy chief or ad manager, you're not involved in budget-making. Nevertheless, it's always helpful to know where the money comes from to pay for the ads you write.

Then when a buyer hates an ad and screams at you "It's my money. I won't pay for it", you can calmly answer back, "It's the store's money and we both work for the same store."

Where **does** the money come from?

Most large stores plan an advertising budget twice a year. The president, the comptroller, and the senior executives, including the sales promotion director, decide how much will be spent on advertising. Depending on how much business they expect the store to do (the money boys call this anticipated volume), fixed events (for example: storewide sales, Mother's Day, the opening of a new branch store), marketing conditions, merchandise emphasis, the amount of vendor money they expect, etc.

This money is then divided among the senior merchants, again depending on past, present, and future factors that affect the amount of advertising during the period. They, in turn, dole the dollars out to buyers. Who request ads and "pay" for them with this money.

The sales promotion director has his own budget. Which covers your salary and a lot of other advertising department expenses, down to your typewriter ribbon and the layout pads in the art department. If money is set aside for institutional ads, it normally goes into this budget and the sales promotion director uses it at his discretion.

This is a very simplified version of a very complex operation. Just enough to give you some idea of the flow of money and where it comes from. The system is not as inflexible as it sounds. The ad budget is usually reviewed monthly and adjusted if necessary. Everybody always seems to have an emergency reserve, a kitty to cover the unexpected. And if there really is no money in the budget for something important, anyone from a buyer to your boss can ask for a budget amendment. Which he'll get if he can justify it.

Budget-making in a small store is, of course, simpler, less formal. Often the boss acts as though the money is coming out of his pocket. It may even be that it is!

More likely, the boss and the ad man sit down and draw up a 3 or 6 month calendar. They decide how much should be spent in each medium. They estimate production and salary costs. They set aside that all-important and ubiquitous kitty. They total it, then add or subtract (it's almost always subtract) to make it come out even with whatever percentage of the sales volume plan they feel is right.

That's the dollar budget. How much can be spent for the period and where it should be spent. After the fixed events and such are entered on the calendar, the buyers troop in. One by one, they tell what they've bought or are buying, how much promotion they need for these stories, where they'd like to run them, and how much vendor support they expect.

These are entered on the calendar and, again, there's a lot of crossing out and cutting space till the figures come out right... matching the dollar budget. Each buyer then knows how much he or she has for the period and is more or less committed to how that money will be spent. More or less because all budgets are fluid. They have to be. We're in a fluid business. If a category suddenly emerges... say, jogging suits, it doesn't make sense to ignore it because ads for the category were not planned months ago when the budget was drawn up.

Be warned, however, that many smaller stores don't plan or budget at all. The boss decides that there will be 3 ads a week, usually because that's what the store has always had. Or he's bought a newspaper contract for that. The cost of those 3 ads x 52 weeks is the budget.

Anywhere from a couple of days to a couple of weeks in advance, the boss and the buyers decide which department and which item will be in the paper. An item they think will pull. If sundresses are hot or solar heaters, or whatever, that's what's advertised during that week.

This is a very bad and un-business-like way to operate, but hundreds and hundreds of small stores around the country are without any advertising plan at all. Stores like these often don't even have a schedule. How can they if they don't know what they'll advertise next week?

CHAPTER 25
THE TALK OF THE TRADE

Like all businesses, advertising has its own specialized language. Much of it is technical terminology that you don't have to know. But there are other words and acronyms that are used frequently. It's a good idea to have some idea of what they mean. Or you may find yourself in the position of an ad manager who took me aside at a meeting and asked me (after swearing me to strict confidence) what a velox really was! He'd been afraid to ask when he was a copy cub. Now he was ashamed to admit he didn't know.

Here, therefore, are some of the words you're most likely to hear during your working hours. From print and broadcast vocabularies. So you can bandy them with the best.

I've skipped terms that are clearly defined in the text of this book and others that take just a little common sense to figure out. The list is far from complete, of course. It could run for many pages. The important thing to remember is that when you hear a word or expression you don't understand, ask what it means. Nobody expects a beginner to know everything. And this is the only way you'll ever learn.

Agate Line. This is the basic measurement used by newspapers. It's one column wide and one-fourteenth of an inch deep. It's usually referred to just as "line" (as in a "250 line ad").

Answer print. The TV equivalent of a proof. It's the first complete print from the negative. If it's approved, it becomes the release print.

Benday. This is often (and perhaps more correctly) spelled Ben Day, after the man who developed it. Benday is a mechanical process that lets the engraver put gray tones and textures on a line drawing. If you look at a Bendayed piece of art in the paper through a magnifying glass, you'll discover that the gray areas are not solid gray at all but made up of myriad individual dots.

Bleed. In print: when the artwork is done larger than the page it's going to be on, then cut back, that's bleed. In other words, wall-to-wall without margins. This is more often a magazine technique than newspaper. In TV: bleed is the amount that can be cut from a picture without losing the message.

BTA. Best Time Available. The station schedules the spots whenever they have a time slot open. If better times open up, the spots are upgraded.

Comp. Short for "Comprehensive". This is a very detailed hand-made version of an ad showing the way it will look in the paper.

CPM. Another of those broadcast acronyms. Cost per M (thousand). What it costs to reach 1000 homes or people. If your rate is $100 dollars for a spot and you reach 10,000 people, your CPM is 1¢.

Cromolite. A chemical used by artists instead of water when they do wash drawings. The engraver sprays it with another chemical and the result is much better reproduction in the paper. (When artwork comes back from the printer and it's turned yellow, it's had the cromolite treatment.)

Cume. Cumulative audience. The total number reached by a station over a period of time. This can be part of a day, a day, or even a week. Depending.

Cut. All artwork in the newspaper is referred to as cuts. Whether they're drawings or photographs.

Demographics. This is really a marketing word, but it's crept into the advertising vocabulary. It refers to the breakdown of readers, audience, customers . . . or whatever you're measuring . . . by age or income or occupation or education, etc.

DT. Double truck. Two facing pages that are normally handled as one, even though the gutter (see below) runs between them. If you're writing a heading for a double truck, try not to divide it into two even parts. **Make** the eye jump the gutter by continuing your statement on the other side.

Flight. An intensive broadcast campaign in a concentrated period of time, usually with a single idea or theme.

Frequency. Another broadcast term. The average number of times a message reaches an unduplicated audience.

GRP. Gross Rating Points. The audiences for each commercial in a schedule.

Gutter. The blank space on the inside margins of the newspaper.

ID. A 10-second spot. This is also used to mean "station identification".

Leading. The space between lines of type is created by strips of lead. If you ask for more leading, they add more strips.

Line cut. This is an engraving where the lines or areas are solid black. A line cut can be art or type. Some papers will gray any line or area larger than the amount they've decided will look nice in the paper. So it won't be a dirty sheet.

Line-for-line. When you want your copy set exactly as you wrote it, each line ending where you have ended it, you ask it to be set line-for-line.

Logo. This is short for the logotype or signature cut of your store ... or the vendor who's footing the bill. The name.

Lucy. She's not a girl, but a pet name for camera lucida. A gadget used by artists and designers that can copy, reduce, and even reverse the artwork that's being copied.

Mechanical. This is an ad that's ready for the camera. Every element has been pasted into position, ready for the engraver in one piece.

Mortice. As a noun: a white area cut out of the artwork or a gray background, usually so type can be set in it. As a verb: to do same.

Open end. A taped commercial that leaves room at the end for a store logo (TV) or store identification (radio).

Preferred position. Page 2 or 3 or other desirable spot in the paper. Which often charges a premium for it.

Reach. The number of different individuals a commercial (or program) reaches. It can be measured for a particular time slot or combination of slots.

Remote. Any broadcast that isn't done in the station's studio.

Retouch. What the retouchers does to a photograph so it will look better and print better. Creases can be erased, a hemline straightened out, and all kinds of small miracles worked with an airbrush. However, too much retouching can make a photograph look hard-boiled.

Reverse type. White type on black or gray.

ROP. Run-of-paper. The ad can appear anywhere in the general section of the paper. However, if your store is a large or steady advertiser, you often get to "own" certain positions; get them day after day. But pay only ROP rates.

ROS. The broadcast equivalent of ROP. A commercial that can be run whenever the station has time open.

Saturation. Heavy use of broadcast in a short period of time. There's vertical saturation (spots all day long to reach everyone) and vertical (spots at the same time for several days to hit the audience that listens at that time).

Square half-tone. Which can be any shape, despite its name, from square to round. What makes it a square half-tone is that the entire area of the artwork is covered with gray dots. Translated from gray tones on the drawing or photo. Half-tones also come in silhouette half-tones (dots in an irregular shape following the silhouette of the artwork) and combination line and half-tone (black areas solid, but the rest translated into gray dots).

Story board. A series of pictures showing the sequence of a TV commercial.

Surprint. Black type superimposed on artwork or a gray background.

Sync. Short for synchronized. When the TV sound is matched to the picture and you can see who's talking. "Voice over", of course, is the sound of an invisible narrator.

Tailor. Cutting or adding copy so it fits the space that it's supposed to fit.

Velox. Its full name is Velox print. It's a photographic copy of the artwork scaled to size. It can be larger than the original or smaller Often it is screened so that it can be rephotographed and reproduced as line copy thereby reducing engraving charges.

Wait order. An ad that's been set but is waiting at the paper for further instructions. The store is sent a proof called, as you'd expect, a wait order proof. Although this whole operation sometimes goes by the name of Display Order.

Widow. When you pick up a widow, you don't go to a singles bar. You cut the single word or two left dangling at the end of a paragraph so the copy block can be neatly squared off. You can also add, if there's enough depth.

CHAPTER 26

BE STRONG — BE PROFESSIONAL

Being a successful copywriter is an attitude as well as a skill. So may I end by giving you some miscellaneous advice?

You can usually make your copy idea work. Once in a while you can't, no matter how much you try. So don't fall in love with an idea (or a word or a phrase). If you have to force the copy to justify a headline, or the idea prevents you from getting across the selling points of your merchandise, scrap it. Start again.

But don't throw it away. If an idea won't work today, it may work tomorrow or next year or on your next job. Most copywriters have trunks full of ideas that someday, somehow, somewhere they may use. Through 10 Bamberger semi-annual furniture sales, I tried to use the no SRO concept (Standing Room Only — a familiar sign at Broadway hit shows). There was always some more important story to tell. Five years later, I gave it to one of my writers at Gimbels who wailed that there was no central theme for a chair ad she was writing. It became her subhead.

Don't pick up and repeat last month's umbrella ad because they only have one little ad a month, so who wants to bother? (Unless the ad was a real winner.) To the umbrella buyer, that's the most important ad in the paper. And the umbrella buyer deserves your best, just as much as the sportswear buyer who has an ad every time you look up. I'll never forget a cub writer who, for six months, wrote a different small ad every week for the pet shop. One canary, one dog bed, 2 dog coats. He now has his own booming ad agency.

Some people still confuse talent and temperament. Let your professionalism surprise them. Have no pride in authorship. Don't flinch visibly when one of your precious words is attacked. *Argue for your copy, not because it's your copy, but because it's right.* Don't get defensive, don't try to justify it if you even suspect you may be wrong. Go back to your typewriter. If a change is necessary, no matter why, be gracious about it. And, on the same subject...when you have to say "no", to a merchant, to an artist...say it gently. "That's a good idea...but".

Don't blame the buyer if an ad flops. Yes, it may be the merchants' fault, but let them bury their mistakes quietly. Besides...who knows...if you had written...

Don't try to remake your store; make the most of it. If you think the merchandise is shoddy or overpriced, and you don't like the store's policy or its attitude...well, you can always go job-hunting.

Watch out for mother-in-law research. Nobody you know orders shoes by mail, so you don't see why you must have a mail and phone line cluttering up your beautiful ad. Yield the point, and you may be surprised by a batch of mail orders. Not from *your* mother-in-law. Not from *your* friends. But those other people.

Expect emergencies. The fashion that takes off...and they want an ad in tomorrow's papers. The buyer who gets a deal on men's pajamas 3 days before Father's Day. The sale that dropped dead because of a snow storm, and they decide to extend it another week. The last-minute sale booklet because the store needs added volume. The merchandise that got lost on its way in, so a new ad must be written. You have to write these emergencies in a hurry and somehow they're usually great. You don't stop to ponder your words. . .you just go.

Don't be drawn into creating by committee. Discussion, yes. Tossing ideas around, yes. But doing an ad is a personal, private matter between you and your typewriter.

Work in whatever way suits you. Do you prefer to write a rough draft in pencil? Do you think on the typewriter? Do you write, then edit...or do you write, then rewrite? There are no rules.

Learn to cut your copy without pain. You may think it will hurt less if somebody else does it. It doesn't. It hurts more.

Adjectives go first. Then re-examine your lead sentence and your last sentence. They're usually the ones that can be tightened most easily.

Take out anything that shows in the illustration, unless you're using it to make a point. Cut out transitions, unnecessary "thats", "howevers". If the copy is still not short enough, it's better to rewrite than to garble what you have.

CHAPTER 27
POSTSCRIPT FOR STUDENTS

There are 3 major users of copywriters: retail stores, advertising agencies, and mail order houses. Manufacturers, newspapers and magazines, and broadcast organizations sometimes use copywriters, but rarely beginners.

Each has its advantages. You may get a larger starting salary at an agency, but you can move up faster in a store. You may have a nicer office in an agency, but at a store or mail order house, you'll get a chance to write more, and write about different kinds of things. (Sinclair Lewis once said that if you want to be a writer, get the hell out and write. It's still good advice.)

When you apply for your first job, bring samples of what you've written, printed or in typed manuscript. Bring ads, stories in the school paper, verse, essays...anything. You can't expect the person interviewing you to judge your writing without seeing it.

If you don't have samples, create some. But, whatever you do, don't rewrite the ads of the store or agency you're going to see. The person you talk to may have done them. Rewrite somebody else's ads. If you really want to be impressive, add a paragraph explaining why you have done the ad the way you have.

Send or bring a resume. A brief well-written carefully typed one that gives the facts. It's not literature, but even a resume can have style.

Try to get the name of an operating person to see. The group chief or copy chief at an agency. The ad manager or copy chief at a store or mail order house. This is usually more productive than working through Personnel. If an operating person thinks you're a genius, a temporary slot may be found for you until a regular job opens up.

And good luck!

INDEX

anniversaries 63,66,68
annual sales 63,66,67,68,89
art and layout 12,16,44,74,79-82
audiences 6,25,26,54,67,68,83,87,107
avoiding generalities 27,28,54,61,71,88,98

base lines 19,57
believability 7,48,49,50
body copy 18,43,44,45,60,61
booklet covers 102,103
branch stores 72,73
broadcast 83-92,93-99
budgets 121,122,123
bullet copy 35
business 121-123
buyers 11,12,110,112,113,114

calendar 122
campaigns 59-62,63,64,86,87,88
captions 19,60,61,101
catalogues 100-107
character count 21, 22
checking facts 11, 23, 24, 30, 31, 32, 40, 43, 113, 114, 115
Christmas 63-66, 96, 97, 102
cliches 34, 39
cold type 20
commercials 83-92, 93-99
comparatives 7, 11, 31, 32, 50
computers 13, 106
consumers 30-32
co-op copy 117-120
copy as salesmanship 1, 2, 7, 93, 100, 101, 103
copy tricks 25-29, 34-36, 39-42, 56, 71, 112, 119
customer benefits 3, 4, 12, 16, 44, 46, 69, 70, 86, 87, 96, 101, 102, 103, 104, 117
customer identification 13, 24, 25, 26, 54, 72
cutting copy 44, 114, 115, 130, 131

demographics 83, 95, 106, 109
details 18, 19, 35, 41
direct mail 100-107
discount stores 70, 71, 72
don'ts 39-40
do's 40-42

editorials 57, 104
emergencies 130
emphasis 79, 80, 90, 94, 114
exaggeration 15, 39, 40

fashion copy 6, 7, 10, 25, 34, 51, 59, 60, 61, 73, 74, 101, 106
first job 132
formats 29, 81

glossary 124-128
grand openings 68, 69, 86

hard sell 46, 47
headlines 3, 12, 13, 15, 16, 17, 28, 45, 63, 64, 65, 66, 103, 119
hot type 20

ideas in copy 9-14, 26, 45, 46, 49, 50, 129, 130
image 52-58, 97
information sheets 112, 113
inserts 100, 101
institutional copy 7, 8, 52, 53, 54, 55, 56, 63

jingles 91, 92

language 10, 25-29, 31, 32, 33-38, 41, 42, 60, 83, 93, 94, 111, 112, 114, 118, 119
layout and art 12, 16, 44, 73, 74, 79-82
lead-ins 17, 18, 64, 65, 84, 87, 88, 112
letters 106, 107, 112
long copy 43, 44, 79

mail order 100-107
management 52, 113, 121-123
manufacturer's aids 24, 32, 118, 119
marketing 108, 109
mats 117, 118
measuring results 2, 3, 8
merchandise experience 9, 10, 11, 12, 112, 113
money 121, 122
music 91, 92

national advertising 6, 132
negatives 34
news in copy 5, 6, 56, 62, 86, 95, 96
newspaper sizes 22, 23

okays 114, 115, 116

phone orders 100-107
photography 20
posters 110, 111
press release 75, 76, 77
principles 3, 4, 5, 11, 13, 25, 26, 27, 39-42, 46, 47, 83, 84, 94, 95, 101, 102, 110, 111, 112
private sales 107
proofreaders' marks 115, 116
proofs 114, 115, 116
public relations 75, 76, 77, 78
punctuation 35, 36

radio 83, 92
reference works 23, 24
restrictions 30, 31, 32, 118, 119

sale copy 7, 46, 48-51, 66-69, 70, 71, 72, 88, 89, 90, 97, 98, 102, 103, 104, 105, 107, 113
schedules 80, 121-123
sections 100, 101
sentences 35, 36, 42, 110, 112
shopping centers 106
short copy 16, 43, 44, 74, 83, 84, 94, 101, 104, 105, 110, 111
simplicity 48, 51, 57
slogans 58
special events 77, 78, 107
specialty shops 10, 73, 74
statistics 109
store superiority 2, 3, 12, 54, 64, 65, 66, 67, 104
students 132
sub-heads 17, 65, 66

taped commercials 90, 91
television 93-99
testing copy 3, 118, 119
timeliness 26-28, 33, 34, 56
type 20, 21, 80, 81

urgency 38, 42, 46, 47, 48, 50, 88, 98, 99

vendor paid advertising 117-120

window signs 111, 112
words 5, 31, 33-38, 39, 40, 41, 60, 83, 84, 92, 94, 95, 111, 114, 115

you approach 14, 25, 26, 40, 41, 101, 102, 109

ABOUT THE AUTHOR:

Judy Young Ocko says that Bernice Fitzgibbon gave her a job at Gimbels because she had a Phi Beta Kappa key and a Ph.D. in Archaeology. These were unusual credits for a writer, but Fitz's instinct was correct. Mrs. Ocko crossed the Hudson from Gimbels to be home furnishings copywriter at Bamberger's, then switched to cosmetics writing at an ad agency. After a stint as group chief at Macy*s, she returned to Gimbels as copy chief.

Now a free lance consultant as well as writer, her clients have ranged from Macy*s, for whom she used to do about 100 ads a year, to small specialty stores, from ad agencies and TV studios to a meat packer and a symphony orchestra. She runs clinics and lectures around the country and teaches at the Tobe-Coburn School for Fashion Careers. In 1974, she was elected to the Retail Advertising Hall of Fame. Behind a typewriter, she is usually known as Judy Young but her full name is Thelma Judith Young Ocko. She is married to a physician, lives in New York City, and has a week-end house in northern New Jersey.

Other books on retail advertising, all published by the NRMA:

Ocko and Rosenblum: "The Secret Ingredient of Good Retail
                       Ads: a Handbook for Buyers
                       and their Bosses"
Ocko and Rosenblum: "The Specialty Store and its Advertising"
Ocko and Rosenblum: "How to be a Retail Advertising Pro"